CONTENTS

INTRODUCTION

College can be expensive, not only because of tuition, but because you're on your own and trying to figure out a food budget, maybe for the first time. You are also probably working with a small kitchen, so storing a bunch of food isn't convenient. In the opening chapters, you'll see what goes into cooking in college and what kind of equipment/food items you'll need. After learning about meal-planning, budgeting, food storage, and safety, we'll get into the recipes.

The recipes only use five ingredients. I don't count water, salt, and pepper among the five, because other 5-ingredient cookbooks don't, and they are so essential to basic flavor and cooking. If I counted them in the five ingredients, there wouldn't be room for other spices or ingredients that make each dish unique. That being said, many of these recipes are truly just five ingredients, even with salt and/or pepper. I've tried to structure the ingredient lists in a way that's understandable.

The recipe sections are divided into:

Breakfast

Salads + Sandwiches

Poultry

Beef + Pork

Seafood

Soups + Stews

Vegan

Snacks

Drinks

Desserts

At the very end of the book, I've included some useful conversion charts you can keep referring to as you cook. Whether you're a home cook just starting out or confident you know your way around a kitchen, these are fast, (usually) healthy, and versatile recipes.

CHAPTER 1: BASIC COOKING TERMS AND SKILLS

Before we get into the nitty-gritty of college cooking, let's review the essentials. If you're brand-new to cooking, however, what are the basic terms and skills you need to know? In this chapter, we'll run down the most important cooking/prepping terms you'll come across in recipes, as well as the must-know knife cuts.

Good-to-know cooking terms

Throughout the recipes in this book (and every other cookbook you might come across), there will be certain terms used to describe prepping and cooking steps. Here's a list of the most common:

Al dente

This Italian phrase refers to the texture of pasta. It literally translates into "to the tooth," meaning your pasta still has a little bite to it, so it isn't soft and mushy. On the back of pasta boxes, there will usually be a suggested time for al dente noodles.

Bake

You bake food in the oven, so it gets cooked using a dry heat. When baking something like a casserole or meat, the recipe might ask that you cover it with foil or a lid.

Baste

When you're cooking meat, usually roasting or grilling, the top can get dried up. This is when you'll "baste," which means brushing the top of the meat with a sauce or marinade during the cooking process.

Beat

This is a pretty self-explanatory term, and usually refers to eggs. When you're asked to "beat" them, it just means whisking them with a whisk or fork until the yolks and whites are blended together. Depending on the recipe, you might beat yolks or whites separately.

Blanch

Blanching is when you cook vegetables (and sometimes fruit) very quickly in hot water, keeping them submerged for just a minute or so, and then dunking them in ice water to stop the cooking process. If you're freezing fresh vegetables, you'll often blanch them first.

Boil

This refers to the temperature of a liquid. You can eyeball it. A "rolling boil" is a very strong boil, with steam rising, while "just boiling" means the water is just starting to consistently bubble.

Braising

Braising is done using wet and dry heat. First, the food gets sautéed at a high temperature (that's the dry heat), and then put into a pot with some liquid. This pot is covered, and the food finishes cooking at a lower temperature. It's a slow-cooking technique.

Caramelize

Caramelizing a food (like onions) means cooking them until they become brown, but not burned. The browning occurs when the carbs and sugar in a food get heated to 300-degrees °F or higher.

Chop

You know what "chopping" means - it's just cutting stuff - so you really just want to look at the word that comes after or before it. You'll be asked to "finely" or "roughly" chop stuff like vegetables and fruit. There's a little more to know about chopping, but we'll get into that when we talk about knife skills shortly.

Cream

This term is used a lot in baking, and refers to how you mix butter and sugar together. You know they're combined properly when the mixture is light and fluffy.

Cut in

When you come across this term, it means to incorporate solid butter into flour, until you get a texture like coarse sand, with little pieces of butter. It's often done with forks, two knives, a pastry cutter, or even your hands.

Deglaze

In recipes, you might be asked to "deglaze" a pan. This means adding a liquid of some kind, like broth or wine, so the stuck-on bits of food dissolve into the liquid. Often times, you'll make a sauce from this delicious mixture.

Dice

When you're asked to "dice" something, imagine what dice look like. The recipe wants you to chop the food into small, even cubes.

Egg wash

An egg wash is when you mix beaten eggs and water or milk. This is then brushed on top of baked goods like pies or pastries, so when baked, there's a shiny glaze on top.

Emulsify

You'll see this word a lot in recipes for homemade salad dressings. Emulsifying is used to create an "emulsion," which is a mixture of liquids that don't blend together naturally, like oil and vinegar. Usually, you'll emulsify by slowly mixing the two liquids drop by drop, whisking quickly, or using a food processor blender.

Filleting

I won't be asking you to remove bones from anything in this cookbook, but just for your general knowledge, filleting refers to how you cut a fish to remove its bones.

Julienne

If you've gotten a veggie cup from a place like Starbucks or somewhere, the vegetables have probably been julienned. This is a knife cut where the veggies are cut into long, even strips. It's the best way to cut veggies if you're making a snack platter with dips.

Marinate

Marinating means letting a meat, fish, veggie, or full meal soak in a sauce (also known as a marinade) to absorb flavors. It's often done for a few hours or even overnight, but there are quick marinades, too. You'll keep the food in the fridge during this process.

Mince

Mincing is basically a very small chop. Garlic and ginger are usually minced, and because the pieces end up so small, you don't have to worry about them all being the same size. You can even mince a food by quickly pulsing it through the food processor a time or two.

Poach

Poaching means letting a food (like chicken or fish) slowly and gently cook in a just-simmering liquid. You've probably eaten a poached egg at some point, which is when you crack an egg into a pot of simmering water and let it cook until it's just done. You can poach meats in milk, too, for a more flavorful result.

Puree

To puree a food, you run it through a blender or food processor until it's perfectly smooth or creamy. Potatoes are often pureed instead of just mashed, so they're lump-free. Pureeing vegetables or fruit also makes very good sauces or toppings for meals.

Roasting

Roasting is similar to baking in that both are done in the oven. However, roasting is typically performed at a higher temperature. Roasted foods are also generally not ever covered, but the main difference is the temperature.

Sauté

To sauté, you heat a skillet or pan, usually with oil, and then cook food like bacon or vegetables relatively quickly, until browned. This ensures really good flavor.

Seasoné

Seasoning is very important in cooking, and in this book, I'll always tell you what spices to use. We aren't counting salt and pepper in the five ingredients, because everyone should have them and most cookbooks with a limited number of ingredients don't count them towards their total. We *do* count anything else, like ground garlic, paprika, and so on.

Simmer

When a liquid is heated, simmering is the first sign that it's getting hot. The water is just starting to move, but not bubbled up quite yet. You gently cook more delicate foods with a simmer.

Slice

Slicing something is a more cautious task than chopping. With slicing, you actually cut your food (like chicken, veggies, fruit, etc.) into even strips. As an example, when slicing a tomato, you get those nice round circles you would put in a burger or sandwich.

Steaming

When steaming, you're actually using very hot steam to cook food. This is a moist heat, as opposed to the dry heat of an oven. Many recipes from Asia use steaming, and you can even buy a steamer just for the purpose. Steaming is often better than boiling, in terms of retaining nutrition.

Stiff peaks

This is another baking term. If instructed to egg whites or cream to "stiff peaks," it means whisking them until the mixture stands up straight when you turn the whisk upside down. Unless you're making meringue, you probably won't need to beat anything into stiff peaks.

Stir-frying

A Chinese cooking method, stir-frying is when you fry ingredients in very hot oil, stirring the whole time so nothing burns. It's most easily done in a wok, but you can stir-fry in a flat, wide pan, too.

Soften

You'll see this term referring to butter when baking. It just means butter that's been brought to room temperature. Since baking is an exact science, it's very important that if a recipe calls for softened butter, you soften it.

Knife cuts to know

Learning the different knife cuts may seem like extra work, but knife skills are the foundation of good prep and cooking. When you've prepared food properly, the final result always turns out better. You'll also stay safer when you're handling knives the right way. Speaking of handling knives, let's first walk through how to hold a knife. You want your pointer finger and thumb at the base of the knife, with your other fingers wrapped around the handle. This ensures a firm grip and control. You'll be tempted to stick out your pointer finger on the backbone of the knife, so watch yourself.

When you actually start chopping or dicing or whatever, the fingers of your *other* hand, which is supporting the cutting board or whatever you're chopping, should be curled into a claw. This way, your fingertips won't get in the way of the blade.

The slice

This basic knife cut is good for slicing large veggies and meat. Begin by holding your knife properly, then putting the tip of the blade against the cutting board (in front of the thing you're slicing), angling the knife upward a little. Now, pull the knife backward while pushing down, slicing through the food. Repeat until you've finished slicing. This cut is almost like you're making a circle with the knife as you go back and forth.

The chop

As we mentioned earlier, chopping is just cutting food up into squares. You will need a very sharp knife, so be careful. Put your food on your cutting board and hold it steady with your claw hand. Keep the knife off the cutting board, above the food at a horizontal angle. Now, push downward into the food, moving the knife a little bit forward as you do so. The chop and slice can be used interchangeably, if you want.

What's the difference between chopping and dicing?

You'll notice we don't have a "dice" knife cut. That's because it's basically the chop, only more precise. When you're just chopping, you don't have to worry about getting everything the same size. With dicing, however, you do want to try and get the pieces very even and according to the size the recipe calls for, i.e. large dice, medium dice, or small dice etc. You'll use either the slice or chop knife cut to accomplish this.

The rock-chop/mince

When you need to mince something, like garlic, ginger, or herbs, the rock-chop is a good knife cut. For a really nice mince, you actually want to first prep the ingredient with a normal chop or slice. This gets it to a good size. Now, shuffle the food into a neat little pile, and put the tip of the knife on top. Put your other hand (the hand that is usually a claw) on the tip of the knife, like your hands are riding a knife see-saw. Now, just start rocking the knife back and forth through the food. Repeat until you have small, minced pieces.

Chiffonade/ribbon cut

This very fancy-sounding name is actually pretty easy. It's used mostly for fresh herbs, so depending on your love of herbs and their availability, you may not use this cut a lot just yet. It's still good to know, though. Begin by stacking up the herb leaves and rolling them from the top down, like you were rolling a cigarette. Now, just carefully slice, so you end up with ribbons of herbs.

Julienne/matchstick cut

The best way to get the classic veggie-tray look is to begin by cutting your carrots, celery, what have you, into 2-inch pieces. Now, turn them so the short end is facing you, and slice down as thin as you can, about ⅛-inch. Once that's done, stack the veggies together and cut lengthwise again, so you end up with very thin, matchstick-like vegetables.

CHAPTER 2: COOKING IN COLLEGE

Being in college is a big adjustment. Depending on how you were raised, you might be responsible for finding your own food for the first time. Even if you are a somewhat experienced cook, you will probably be adjusting to much smaller spaces and a more limited budget. In this chapter, let's break down what cooking in college can be like, whether you're in a dorm or off-campus.

On-campus versus off-campus living

The college experience will most likely be divided between dorm living and off-campus living. This isn't always the case, since some students stay on campus their whole college career or rent off-campus with roommates. You may even not leave home for whatever reason, and commute to class. That's still basically just two options, however - on campus or off - and cooking will be different for both.

On-campus

When you're on campus in a dorm, you may not have access to a full kitchen whenever you want. Odds are, your dorm will have a kitchenette of some kind, with a microwave, stovetop, and oven. Depending on the college, you may be allowed to bring your own appliances from home (like a smoothie blender or rice cooker), as long as you don't use it in your room. Find out from your RA if that's allowed. If it's not, you'll be limited to that communal microwave, stovetop, and oven. As for a fridge and freezer, there may be one in the common area, but you might not be comfortable leaving your food unguarded. A personal mini fridge in your room is the way to go. You'll have limited space, which affects how much refrigerated or frozen stuff you can buy, and how much leftovers you can keep.

On-campus cooking may not necessarily be relegated to a tiny dorm kitchen, however. If you're involved in campus life and activities, you will probably find spaces with larger kitchens. You could also potentially make friends with students living in houses close by. If you ask nicely and offer some kind of payment as a thank you (making food is always a popular sign of gratitude), they might let you use their kitchen to prep a few days' worth of meals or keep leftovers in their freezer/fridge. If you're on-campus, be on the lookout for these opportunities.

Off-campus

Your college cooking options expand significantly if you live off-campus. Before making a commitment to a house or apartment, make sure you know what will be waiting for in the kitchen. Does the place come with a microwave or will you have to bring your own? What's the counter and cupboard space like? Having a clear picture and knowing what to expect will make the transition easier.

With a larger kitchen that you don't have to share with an entire dorm floor, you'll be able to buy more appliances like a multi-cooker or blender, if you can afford them. Extra space doesn't mean extra money, so bear that in mind when grocery-shopping. You still want to meal-plan and be on the lookout for sales. If you're living off-campus your whole college career, the same rules apply.

Cooking considerations

Regardless of where you're living, it's good to keep certain considerations in mind when shopping, meal-planning, and cooking. Here are some questions to keep asking yourself:

What's my food budget for the week/month?

What meals am I making this week?

What snacks am I eating this week?

Do I have space in my fridge/freezer/cupboards for the food I'm buying?

Do I feel good (healthwise) about the food choices I'm making?

Do I want to double or triple the recipe I'm making so I can have leftovers?

What appliances can I really not live without?

Is there a way I could be saving money on groceries?

Do I have time this week to make the food I planned?

You don't need to agonize over these questions 24/7, but keeping them at the back of your mind will help you stay on track – healthwise, budgetwise, spacewise, and timewise. You'll be more organized and feel in control, which is important during stressful times in college like the first year, finals, and thinking about graduation. Hopefully you'll have the answers to at least two of these questions - what meals and snacks you're eating this week - by continuing to read this book.

CHAPTER 3: KITCHEN TOOLS AND PANTRY-STACKING

In this chapter, we're getting into all the equipment you absolutely need to cook in college. We'll also talk about the equipment that's really nice to have, and will let you make absolutely *all* the recipes in this book. If you live in a dorm room, you should ask your RA about some of the equipment (like a smoothie blender and multi-cooker), but if you live off-campus, you should definitely consider getting everything. We'll also get into how to stock your pantry, fridge, and freezer. Let's start with equipment, first:

Must-have cooking equipment

To cook most recipes in this book, you'll need the following equipment. Take note: I'm not counting bowls, spoons, forks, cups, etc. You don't really "cook" in those.

Meat thermometer

Eating undercooked meat is not only unpleasant, it's dangerous. You need a good, reliable meat thermometer as part of your college cooking arsenal.

A decent knife set

To prep and chop stuff, you need knives, and you can find decent sets for $20-$25.

Cutting board

Speaking of cutting, you'll need a board. Avoid plastic if you can, because little pieces can get in your food.

Stovetop pots

I recommend at least two stovetop pots: one big enough to cook pasta and another medium-sized one.

Cast iron skillet

You'll use a skillet a lot for various meals, and I like cast iron, since you can move it from the stove to the oven. You can find a decent one for $25 or so.

Cookie sheets

It's probably a good idea to have at least two cookie sheets. I like ones with rims, because they absorb heat better.

Microwave

Microwaves can be used to quickly cook certain food and heat up leftovers. If you're in a dorm, you'll probably have access to one somewhere. If you're living off-campus, be sure your place has one.

Pizza cutter

Good for slicing certain doughs (like cheese cracker dough in the "Snacks" section) and of course, slicing pizza.

Can opener

A basic tool that's easily forgotten, you'll need it to open cans of beans, corn, etc.

Mini fridge

If you're on campus, you'll need your own mini fridge to store food and leftovers. Prices vary by size.

Measuring cup and measuring spoon set

To measure ingredients, you obviously need a measuring set.

Nice-to-have equipment

There are really just two pieces of equipment that are really nice to have, but aren't absolutely necessary for most of the recipes. If you can, though, I highly-recommend them:

Rice cooker/multi-cooker

A lot of the recipes in this book use rice, and it's way easier to cook rice using a rice cooker than on the stovetop. If you have the space and budget, however, I recommend getting a multi cooker instead. These are three appliances in one: rice cooker, slow cooker, and pressure cooker. You probably can't have one in your dorm, but once you're off-campus, they are a big time-saver.

With slow cookers, you might be tempted to get a big one, just for the future, but if you're cooking meals for just one person, they might not turn out well in a giant cooker. There are a big range of sizes from mini 1.5-quarts to 8+ quarts. For most of the recipes in this book, especially the soups and stews, slow cooker versions should be good in a 2-quart/8-cup cooker.

For *multi-cookers* with pressure cooking settings, however, I actually recommend a 6-quart one, though, which may seem big - it lets you cook up to six servings of rice - but it can also cook much less. On the pressure cooking setting, it only needs ½ - 1 cup of liquid to work. I've successfully cooked just two small chicken breasts in a 6-quart pressure cooker.

Smoothie blender/little food processor

There are a handful of recipes in this book that call for blending. You'll need either a smoothie blender or food processor. These can be found for pretty cheap, so it's just a matter of if your dorm will allow them. Once you're off-campus, do make getting one a priority. If you want to be able to blend frozen things, ice cubes, or harder foods like root veggies, expect to pay a bit more for good blades and power.

Must-have pantry list

You know what equipment you need, but what about actual food? Here's the very bare minimum:

Eggs

Eggs are good on their own and good in both savory and sweet recipes.

Meat

Lots of the recipes in this book use ground meat, like turkey, pork, chicken, and beef, while the poultry section also uses frozen chicken. Since you probably have a small freezer, you may not be able to have a wide variety of meat, but you should always have something on hand.

Bananas

A portable snack, one of the most affordable fruits you can get, and important in a variety of recipes.

Pasta

Pasta is really filling and easy to make, and the base of quite a few recipes.

Rice

Similar to pasta in that it's a very filling ingredient, and in a lot of recipes in the book.

Plain yogurt

A replacement for mayo and sour cream, yogurt is also great for breakfast and dips.

Honey

My favorite sweetener because it lasts forever and is sweeter than sugar, so you don't need a lot when you use it.

Olive oil

A very healthy oil, it's used for pretty much every savory recipe.

Bread

If you're going to make sandwiches or toast, you need bread.

Peanut butter

High in protein, peanut butter is a great snack for any time of the day or night.

Cheese

Good on its own as a snack, mixed into pasta, crumbled on top of salad, or sliced for sandwiches, you can use cheese in a lot of different ways.

Milk

I consider either cow's milk or non-dairy milk an essential fridge ingredient, because it's used in a lot of recipes and drinks, like coffee or tea.

Canned tuna

It doesn't take up shelf space, it lasts forever, and it's packed with protein. While you can't afford a lot of seafood, you can always afford tuna.

Salt and pepper

I don't even count salt and pepper as ingredients in the five-ingredient recipes, because they're both so essential. Without them, food is terribly bland.

Dried garlic

I put dried garlic just under salt and pepper in terms of importance.

Italian seasoning

I couldn't afford a lot of fresh herbs in college, and didn't have space for a bunch of dried ones, so just one good blend of Italian seasoning is the way to get herby flavor.

Paprika

I really like paprika's spice, but if you have another hot spice you prefer (like dried red pepper flakes), go ahead and get that one instead. You need at least one spicier spice in your pantry.

Frozen vegetables

Fresh produce seems to go bad the second you put it on the counter, so frozen is the way to go. Depending on space, try to have at least one bag of frozen veggies at all times.

Canned beans

A good source of protein and fiber, canned beans are very affordable and last a long time. Dry beans are probably cheaper in terms of volume, but they take longer to cook. If you're a vegetarian or vegan, you'll definitely want canned beans around for fast meals.

Canned tomatoes

Canned tomatoes are cheap flavor bombs that can be mixed in rice, pasta, stews, and more. They last a long time and don't need to be refrigerated (unless opened).

Flour

Used to thicken sauces and provide the base of pretty much any baked good, flour is good to have around. All-purpose is fine.

Oats

If you eat a lot of overnight oats like I did in college, you'll always want rolled oats around. They can also be ground into flour with a food processor if needed, or baked into homemade granola.

Nice-to-have food items

The items above are ingredients I think are absolutely essential to any kind of college cooking, but they don't represent everything. The list below describes the food items that are really nice to have around if you want to diversify your cooking and eating lifestyle, but if you don't love them, have the space, or the budget, you can go without them and be just fine.

Avocados

Because of their price and tiny ripeness window, avocados are a nice-to-have item to always have around, and not a must-have. They're good mashed up on toast, in smoothies, sliced on salads and sandwiches, and you can even make chocolate mousse with them.

Jam

I made a lot of overnight oats in college, and I really liked using jam because it provides both sweetness and flavor. If you make a lot of oats or other recipes where you need fruity sweetness, always have jam on hand.

Frozen berries

If you don't make smoothies a lot, you might want to save space in your freezer for other things and skip berries. However, if you live on smoothies for breakfast or a snack, frozen berries will be a must-have. They're also nice to have around as an add-in to yogurt and oatmeal.

Sugar or sugar alternative

I like honey over sugar in general, which is why honey is in the must-have, but sometimes you need granulated sugar for baking. If you're a big cookie maker, you'll want a bag of sugar or a sugar alternative around.

Butter

You always need olive oil, no matter what, but butter is also a great fat to keep close if you have the space. It can be used in a wide variety of sweet and savory recipes.

Pesto

If you make a lot of sandwiches and think mayo is boring, pesto is a great condiment. It's also great mixed into pasta or rice, so if space and budget allows it, I recommend keeping a container in the fridge.

Hummus

I personally had hummus a lot, because I loved it on sandwiches and as a veggie dip, but if you aren't like me, it belongs on the nice-to-have list, as opposed to the "must-have." If you have room and you like it, by all means, keep it around.

Deli turkey

Deli turkey is really versatile and can be used to make sandwiches, snacks, and salads. If you love a good turkey sandwich, you'll want this in your fridge consistently. If not, however, just buy as needed.

Salsa

Great with eggs, potato hashes, and as a snack with chips, salsa packs a lot of flavor in a small container. If you have room in your fridge shelves, I recommend keeping your favorite kind around.

Fresh tomatoes

If you make a lot of sandwiches or salads, a slice of fresh tomato or chopped tomatoes is a great ingredient. If you don't make these meals a lot, however, keeping fresh tomatoes around is probably not necessary. You can just stick with canned.

Lemon/lime

Having a fresh lemon or lime around ensures you can always add a burst of acid to any meal, whether it's fish or a salad. You can also buy pure lemon or lime juice, and it will last longer in the fridge.

Chicken/veggie stock

For most recipes, you just need water, but for the best flavor in a lot of this book's recipes - especially the soups and stews chapter- I recommend chicken stock. In fact, if you make a lot of soups and stews, I would label chicken or veggie stock as a must-have. Stock can be stored in a pantry as long as it's sealed, but once opened, it should go in the fridge.

Leafy greens

If you're a big salad person, you definitely always want greens on hand, but if you aren't, this won't be a "must-have" for you. Greens go bad pretty quickly, so if you don't know for sure you're going to be using them, don't waste your money.

Sweet chili sauce/balsamic salad dressing

A handful of the recipes rely on sweet chili sauce or balsamic for flavorings, so it's nice to have these on hand. You can quickly flavor up plain meat or make simple salads more appealing.

Tortillas

A nice alternative to bread, tortillas can be used for sandwiches, quick tacos, or just plain cheese quesadillas.

How to meal plan

Once you have your pantry stacked, you'll be able to meal plan. While it may take a little bit of work upfront, meal planning actually saves time, energy, and money, which are all things often in short supply for students. The first step is to think simple. Meals don't need to be complicated with lots of ingredients and they don't have to be dramatically different from day to day or week to week. This book uses a lot of the same ingredients over and over again, but thanks to spices and mix-ins, the meals don't get boring.

With "think simple" as your philosophy, plan meals 3-5 days in advance. Snacks should be included, so you never find yourself hungry and without a clue about what to eat. With the meal plan you've designed, see if there's anything you can make in advance, like rice. You don't want to make it too far in advance, which is why 3-5 days is a good schedule. You should also consider if you have space in the fridge for prepped foods. With a meal plan in place, you can go shopping and get everything you need in one trip.

Creating a budget

To cook in college, you'll need a grocery budget. Look at your current finances and see how much you currently spend on food. Is it as low as you want it to be? Examine where the money is going and if there's anything you could eliminate. That money maybe could be going to another ingredient, or back in your pocket. To save money on the food budget, consider switching grocery stores, buying generics only, and buying in bulk. Since you probably don't have the space for giant boxes of food or a million cans, think about asking a friend or two to pitch in, and split up what you buy. After about a month of trying out your budget, take a look back. Think about what worked and what didn't work. It can take a while to get into the swing of things, budget-wise, so don't be discouraged.

If you like apps, there are a handful that can help you with tracking your spending, such as:

Out Of Milk - Shopping list app that you can share with roommates/housemates

Flipp - Helps you find coupons and deals

Grocery IQ - Build grocery lists and tracks what stores have them

Mint - A budgeting app that you can link to your bank account

PocketBudget - A very streamlined, simple budgeting app

CHAPTER 4: FOOD SAFETY AND STORAGE

Food safety isn't the sexy part of cooking, but it's really important, because it can be a matter of life and death. I recently heard a really depressing story about a student who died after eating 5-day old spaghetti. Why did this happen? He left it out at room temperature that whole time. Proper food safety and storage is super important, so we're spending a chapter on it before getting to the recipes.

Safety tips

Since I know you don't want to be flipping back to this section to see how long a meal should be stored, I've told you how to properly store each recipe and how long it should last. For meat-based recipes, I'll also tell you what temperature it should be cooked to, but here's a chart below to get an idea of the temps you want to aim for:

Meat Cooking Temperatures
Beef = 145 °F
Poultry (including chicken sausage) = 165 °F
Sausage (beef, pork, lamb) = 160 °F
Pork = 145 °F
Seafood = 145 °F

Fresh fish, poultry, and ground meat should be eaten or frozen two days after buying, while beef and pork should be eaten or frozen after 3-5 days. Meat should *always* be stored in either the fridge or the freezer. You can expect frozen meats to last anywhere from 1-2 months to a year. It depends on the specific food. Look up the USDA's recommendations on their website.

To thaw, sticking frozen meats in the fridge is the safest method, since it's slow. Just make sure any juice isn't dripping everywhere. If you want to thaw faster outside the fridge, you can put frozen food in a Ziploc plastic bag and submerge in water. According to the USDA, you should change the water every 30 minutes and cook as soon as the meat is thawed.

You should always wash your hands before handling raw meat, and then after handling it. If you don't, you risk cross-contaminating. Always wash knives, utensils, bowls and cutting boards that have come into contact with raw meat. Hot, soapy water does the trick.

Food storage

The containers you use for food storage is important for both food safety and quality. There are so many choices, so consider your needs. Do you want containers to carry lunches around? Small ones will work. If you want to store larger amounts of leftovers, you'll need bigger ones. Plastic is probably the most convenient and most budget-friendly. You'll want a brand that's durable, and be sure it's microwave, freezer, and dishwasher-friendly. Even if you don't currently have a dishwasher, you might someday. To hand-wash plastic containers, just use hot, soapy water. Certain foods may stain, like tomato sauce.

You'll also want a good supply of freezer-safe gallon bags. These take up less room than containers. I also liked having a few glass mason jars around for overnight oats, smoothies, and leftover sauces or dips. You can wash out glass jam jars and reuse them if you don't want to buy all-new jars.

Remember, stay safe

As you cook and store food, always remember to play it safe. If you aren't sure about a leftover, don't eat it. If you do eat something questionable and get sick, don't put off seeking medical attention if you start getting scared. Usually, people recover from food poisoning without much fanfare, but if you ever start experiencing abnormal symptoms like a temperature higher than 100.4 F, extreme pain, and so on (you can check the Mayo Clinic website for more info), get to the ER.

Well, that wasn't necessarily the most pleasant place to jump off from to get into our recipes, but it's important. Read the recipes closely, especially when they start talking about temperatures. Follow the directions, and everything will be fine!

CHAPTER 5: BREAKFAST

The first meal of the day: is it really the most important one? There's still some debate about it, but I know during my college years, I could really tell the difference between eating breakfast and not eating any breakfast. However, I rarely wanted to get up even a few minutes earlier than absolutely necessary, so a lot of these recipes can be prepared in advance. The ones that aren't? As quick and simple as possible. On weekends, when I could be more leisurely, I loved avocado-egg toast, turkey hashes with salsa, or pancakes, so those recipes are here, too.

Peanut Butter + Jelly Overnight Oats

Serves: 1

Time: Overnight

Overnight oats are a really great breakfast for students and anyone who doesn't have much time in the morning. You prep them the night before, stick the container in the fridge, and in the morning, you have a fiber-full breakfast. These oats are enriched with peanut butter for protein, jam for sweetness, and just a pinch of salt to bring all the flavors together.

Tip: *If you want to make this dairy-free, simply substitute regular milk with almond, coconut, or soy milk.*

Ingredients:

½ cup old-fashioned oats

½ cup milk

1 tablespoon peanut butter

1 teaspoon jam of your choice

Pinch of salt

Directions:

Mix oats, milk, and peanut butter together in a Mason jar or another container. Seal and refrigerate overnight. In the morning, stir well, and add jam and salt. Enjoy!

Nutritional Info (1 oats per serving):

Total calories: 283

Carbs: 35

Protein: 13

Fat: 11

Fiber: 5

Strawberry-Coconut Overnight Oats (Vegan)

Serves: 1

Time: Overnight

If you are trying to lower your dairy intake or you're vegan, these oats are the perfect breakfast. The oats are infused with mild sweetness thanks to coconut milk (like So Delicious) and topped with shredded coconut. I like fresh strawberries with this recipe, but you can substitute just about any fruit you have on hand.

Ingredients:

½ cup old-fashioned rolled oats

½ cup coconut milk

Pinch of salt

½ tablespoon shredded coconut

3 large sliced strawberries

Directions:

Mix oats and milk together in a Mason jar or other container. Seal and refrigerate overnight. In the morning, add a little salt and stir. Top with shredded coconut and strawberries.

Nutritional Info (1 oats per serving):

Total calories: 141

Carbs: 23

Protein: 3.1

Fat: 4.6

Fiber: 3.8

Green Smoothie

Serves: 1

Time: About 5 minutes

There's nothing quite as healthy as a green smoothie to start your morning. Even if you don't love green smoothies, this recipe is a good introduction, thanks to a banana for sweetness and protein-packed nut butter. If you want to make more smoothie for later, or you don't finish this serving, it will keep in the fridge in a sealed jar or covered glass for about 12 hours or so.

Tip: *If you use a frozen banana, the smoothie will be colder and thicker. If you aren't sure that your blender is up to pulverising frozen or icy ingredients, just use a fresh banana.*

Ingredients:

1 cup dairy or non-dairy milk

2 cups spinach leaves

2 tablespoons nut butter of your choice (i.e. peanut butter, almond butter, etc.)

½ large banana

Directions:

Pour milk into your blender, then add spinach, nut butter, and banana. Blend until smooth and drink.

Nutritional Info (1 smoothie with cow's milk + peanut butter):

Total calories: 384

Carbs: 36

Protein: 18.5

Fat: 21.6

Fiber: 5

Strawberry-Banana Smoothie

Serves: 1

Time: About 5 minutes

A classic smoothie, strawberries and bananas are full of fiber and other energizing minerals and vitamins. For extra thickness and protein, I'm recommending some plain Greek yogurt in addition to milk. If you don't have any on hand, you can just add more milk. I also like chia seeds in this smoothie, but they're purely optional.

Ingredients:

½ cup dairy or non-dairy milk

¼ cup plain Greek yogurt

1 cup sliced strawberries

½ large banana

1 tablespoon chia seeds (optional)

Directions:

Add ingredients to your smoothie in the order they appear - milk first, then yogurt, strawberries, banana, and chia seeds. If you're using a frozen banana, add that last.

Nutritional Info (1 smoothie w/ cow's milk and chia seeds per serving):

Total calories: 350

Carbs: 48.4

Protein: 16.2

Fat: 12.2

Fiber: 15.7

Berry Yogurt Parfait

Serves: 1

Time: Less than 5 minutes

Yogurt parfaits are a common sight at coffee shops and cafeterias, but they're really easy to make yourself, and you'll save money. In this version, I'm recommending berries, since they are the healthiest fruit. If you decide you don't want to use honey, most people find blueberries sweeter than raspberries or blackberries. A lot of granolas are also fairly sweet, so you might not miss the honey at all if you leave it out. If you can't find 6-ounce containers of just plain yogurt, go with vanilla, and you'll definitely not need the honey.

Tip: *You can use fresh or frozen berries, though if you use frozen, you'll probably want to thaw them a bit before eating. Just run them under water.*

Ingredients:

One 6-ounce container of plain Greek yogurt (like Chobani Plain)

½ tablespoon honey (optional)

¾ cup berries (your choice)

¼ cup granola

Directions:

If you're using honey, mix it into the plain yogurt. Then, put ½ of your berries into the bottom of a glass, and spoon over yogurt. Add more berries, then yogurt again, and top with granola.

Nutritional Info (1 parfait with blueberries):

Total calories: 291

Carbs: 42

Protein: 19.5

Fat: 6.5

Fiber: 3.4

Microwave Oatmeal

Serves: 1

Time: Less than 5 minutes

Overnight oats are great, especially during the warmer months, but when it gets cold, I want hot oatmeal. This oatmeal is cooked quickly in the microwave and it's endlessly customizable, so you can add whatever you want to it, even chocolate (I won't judge).

Tip: *Because this is a quick recipe, you might think you need quick-cooking oats, but you actually don't. Stick with good old-fashioned rolled oats.*

Ingredients:

1 cup milk

½ cup old-fashioned rolled oats

Pinch of salt

1 teaspoon pure vanilla extract

Fruit of your choice (like sliced banana)

Directions:

Mix milk, oats, and salt in a microwave-safe bowl. Cook in the microwave for 2 ½ minutes and stir. If you like softer oats, cook for another 30 seconds. Add vanilla and top with fruit. Dig in!

Nutritional Info (1 oatmeal with ¼ sliced banana):

Total calories: 223

Carbs: 32.2

Protein: 11

Fat: 6.4

Fiber: 2.8

Avocado-Egg Toast

Serves: 1

Time: Less than 10 minutes

Avocado toast gets mocked in some circles, but the reality is, if you like avocado, avocado toast is dang delicious. It gets even more delicious when you add a protein-rich egg. It's a breakfast that requires minimal work and gives you a boost of energy to take on your day.

Tip: *If you don't have access to a toaster for some reason, you can quickly toast bread in the oven using the broiler. Drizzle a little olive oil on the slice and stick in the hot oven for about 1 minute, or until you get the color you want.*

Ingredients:

Splash of olive oil

1 egg

One slice of whole-grain bread

1 small, ripe avocado

Salt to taste

Pinch of pepper

Directions:

Add some olive oil to a skillet and heat on medium. When the oil is hot and shiny, crack the egg in the skillet and cook. I like to cook the egg until it's just starting to change color on the skillet side and get crispy edges, and then flip it and cook for just a few seconds. The yolk won't get hard, but I know for sure the white is cooked through.

While the egg is cooking, keep one eye on the skillet, and the other on the bread. Toast to the color you like. Carefully cut the avocado and remove the skin. The egg should be done by now, so remove from heat. Smash the avocado on the toasted bread, add the egg, and season generously with salt and pepper. Enjoy!

Nutritional Info (1 recipe per serving):

Total calories: 550

Carbs: 24.2

Protein: 11.8

Fat: 47.9

Fiber: 11.7

Turkey-Salsa Hash

Serves: 1

Time: 15-20 minutes

For a hearty breakfast, I really love hashes. They're the perfect combo of eggs, meat, potatoes, and seasonings. It's very easy to mix them up, as well, and swap in different meats and spices. In this recipe, ground turkey is a great choice, and instead of using a bunch of dried spices, we're just going to use salsa. It's a really easy way to add flavor. For the potatoes, I went with frozen hash browns, since they cook fairly quickly. You can find them frozen in most grocery stores. Sometimes you can find them in rectangles, like how McDonald's sells them, and you can cook them in the oven instead of a skillet. It just depends on what your store has.

Ingredients:

Olive oil

1 cup frozen hash browns

¼ pound ground turkey sausage (from a brand like Jennie-O)

½ cup salsa

2 eggs

Salt to taste

Directions:

You'll need two skillets/pans for this recipe - one for the turkey sausage, eggs, and salsa, and the other for the hash browns. Add a splash of oil to both and heat. When the oil is hot and shiny, add hash browns to one skillet (just enough to fit the skillet in a single layer) and ground turkey in the other. Cook both, stirring the meat occasionally, but letting the hash browns cook in a single layer in its skillet. If either starts to look dry, add more oil.

After 5-7 minutes, flip the hash browns, so they can brown on the other side. When the turkey is cooked through and brown, add salsa and stir. Cook for 2-3 minutes, then crack in the eggs. Cover this meat/egg/salsa skillet and cook for 7 minutes, or until the egg whites are a solid color. The hash browns will probably be done first, so move to a plate and cover with a paper towel, so they stay warm.

When everything is cooked, top your hash browns with the meat, egg, and salsa mixture. Season to taste with salt. Enjoy!

Nutritional Info (1 recipe per serving):

Total calories: 694

Carbs: 64.6

Protein: 30.8

Fat: 35.5

Fiber: 7.1

Sausage 'n Egg Muffins

Serves: 3 people or 1 person for 3 days (serving size is 2 muffins)

Time: About 40 minutes

These portable protein bombs are a perfect breakfast and also a snack, if you want them to be. Make the muffins when you have a free hour or so, and you'll have enough for three days, if you're the only one eating them. If you anticipate eating more than two muffins a day, simply double the recipe to make 12 muffins. Store in the fridge no longer than 5-6 days.

Ingredients:

Splash of oil

¼ cup ground pork sausage

4 eggs

½ cup cheddar cheese

Salt to taste

Black pepper to taste

Directions:

Splash a little oil into a skillet and heat until shiny. Add ground sausage and cook until brown. In a bowl, whisk the eggs. Mix in cooked meat, cheese, salt, and pepper. Grease six cups of a muffin tray and pour in egg mixture, so the cups are ⅔ full. Bake at 350-degrees for 30 minutes. To check if the muffins are done, stick a toothpick in the center. It should come out clean.

Nutritional Info (2 muffins):

Total calories: 400

Carbs: 0.7

Protein: 25.4

Fat: 32.1

Fiber: 0

Easiest Skillet Pancakes Ever

Serves: 1

Time: About 10-12 minutes

Pancakes always make me think of lazy Sunday mornings, and waking to the sound of sizzling batter. My younger brother was always the one making them; he had a natural talent for the perfect flapjacks, and my mom loved that she could have a break from the kitchen. This incredibly-simple recipe is sure to make you popular at school, if you make a big batch for your friends, and even if it's just you, you'll feel a little closer to home.

Tip: *You can easily double or triple this recipe, though it will take longer since you can only cook one pancake at a time in a skillet. If you have a larger griddle, great! You'll be able to cook more.*

Ingredients:

1 cup flour

2 eggs

1 cup milk

¼ teaspoon salt

Butter

Fruit of your choice (or maple syrup)

Directions:

Grease a large skillet with butter and heat. While that gets hot, gently mix flour, eggs, milk, and salt together. Mix until the ingredients are just combined, but don't worry about small lumps. Most people overmix pancake batter, and the cakes don't end up as light and fluffy as they should.

Once the batter is ready, pour ¼ cup portions into the hot skillet. Wait until the top is bubbling, and then flip. Cook for another 12 seconds or so, until you get the color you want. Repeat until you've used all the batter.

To serve, top with nubs of butter and slices of your favorite fruit, like bananas or strawberries. You can also use good ol' fashioned maple syrup instead.

Nutritional Info (1 recipe with ½ tablespoon butter, no maple syrup or fruit):

Total calories: 649

Carbs: 96

Protein: 26

Fat: 17

Fiber: 3.4

CHAPTER 6: SALADS & SANDWICHES

A sandwich or salad might be the perfect lunch. There's usually no cooking involved, or very little cooking, and there are so many ways to customize a sandwich or salad. They're also very easy to make as healthy as you want, which is important during college when stress levels are high and you need all the good health you can get. In this section, you'll find recipes for some of my go-to salads and sandwiches during my school years, and the ones I still eat to this day.

Spinach-Pesto Pasta Salad

Serves: 1-2

Time: Less than 20 minutes

I love pesto. It's such a fresh, versatile flavor bomb and it always makes me think of summer. In this recipe, the pesto is basically the "dressing" for a pasta salad, which includes cherry tomatoes, spinach, and plenty of mozzarella. Salads have a reputation for being bland, so be sure to add some salt to bring all the flavors together.

Ingredients:

Water (for boiling)

½ pound dry penne pasta

½ container cherry tomatoes

3 generous handfuls of spinach

Generous handful of shredded mozzarella

6 tablespoons pesto

Salt to taste

Directions:

Cook pasta in boiling water until al dente, according to the package. Drain and turn on the cold water faucet, so the pasta cools down. In a big bowl, mix pasta with tomatoes, spinach, mozzarella, and pesto. Taste and season with salt to your liking. Serve. Leftovers will keep in the fridge for about 3 days.

Nutritional Info (½ recipe):

Total calories: 619

Carbs: 80.8

Protein: 23.1

Fat: 22.9

Fiber: 5.3

Strawberry-Cucumber Salad

Serves: 2 (as a side)

Time: About 5 minutes

I don't think enough people put fruit in green salads. Strawberries are an especially great ingredient because of their sweet-sour flavor, and eye-catching color. You'll be excited to dig in to this salad, which has a Romaine lettuce base, fresh crunchy cucumber, salty Parmesan, and a balsamic salad dressing of your choice. I personally love anything that's balsamic + berries, but if that's too sweet for you, just regular ol' balsamic works great, too.

Tip: *To make this a meal, add cooked chicken.*

Ingredients:

Two generous handfuls of Romaine lettuce

1 chopped cucumber

1 cup chopped strawberries

¼ cup balsamic salad dressing

Handful of shredded Parmesan cheese

Directions:

Toss the lettuce, cucumber, and strawberries together. Drizzle with dressing and top with Parmesan. Serve!

Nutritional Info (½ recipe per serving):

Total calories: 218

Carbs: 25.8

Protein: 5.6

Fat: 11.3

Fiber: 2.7

Black Bean-Bacon Salsa Salad

Serves: 4-6 (depending on if it's the main or a side)

Time: Less than 10 minutes

This started out as a regular salsa with just beans, corn, and tomato, but I wanted to add my own spin. I thought, why not bacon? It makes the dish more robust and means I don't need to add as much salt. I had an avocado lying around, so I cubed that up and threw that in, too. I fell in love after the first bite, and the reason I classify this as both a salsa and a salad, is because I think it's hearty enough to eat on its own, sans chips.

Ingredients:

4 strips of bacon

3 cups diced tomatoes

2 cups canned black beans

½ 14.5-oz can corn kernels

1 cubed avocado

Salt to taste (if needed)

Directions:

Cook bacon to desired crispiness. The juices from the rest of the salad will make the bacon a bit soggy after a while, so a little crisper than your usual liking is a good idea. Next, dice tomatoes, and drain black beans and corn kernels. Dump in a big bowl. Add bacon and cubed avocado. Gently mix to get the flavors blended. Taste, and salt if necessary.

Leftovers will keep for 2 days or so. Avocado will probably brown a little, but still be fine.

Nutritional Info (¼ recipe per serving):

Total calories: 340

Carbs: 23.1

Protein: 10.6

Fat: 24.3

Fiber: 9

Lentil-Tomato Salad (Vegan)

Serves: 2 (as a side)

Time: Less than 5 minutes

Lentils are often called a "superfood," and a quick glance at its nutritional benefits shows why. The legume is high in complex carbs, fiber, folate, magnesium, and more. They're also a favorite protein source for vegetarians and vegans. In this side salad, they combine with sweet cherry tomatoes, sharp balsamic vinegar, dried basil, and salt.

Ingredients:

One 15-oz can of lentils

1 cup cherry tomatoes

Drizzle of balsamic vinegar

Dried basil to taste

Salt to taste

Directions:

Rinse and drain the lentils. Pour into a bowl. Cut the cherry tomatoes in half and add to the bowl. Drizzle with balsamic vinegar. Season with basil and salt to taste.

Leftovers should be refrigerated no longer than 3 days.

Nutritional Info (½ recipe per serving):

Total calories: 264

Carbs: 46.6

Protein: 20.2

Fat: 0.8

Fiber: 17.8

Chicken Salad (With Yogurt)

Serves: 2

Time: 5 minutes (if you've already cooked the chicken or are using a rotisserie) - 25 minutes

Chicken salad is one of the easiest protein-rich meals you can make. A lot of recipes call for mayonnaise, but we're going to use Greek yogurt, which is better for you. Feel free to experiment with this recipe by swapping in cucumber or grapes for celery; or raisins for craisins; or add toasted nuts. Even if you're planning on eating this alone, make the full recipe, and use the salad in sandwiches for the next few days.

Ingredients:

2 cups cooked chicken breast

½ cup chopped celery

¼ cup plain Greek yogurt

¼ cup dried cranberries (optional)

Salt to taste

Black pepper to taste

Tip: *You can buy a whole rotisserie chicken for fairly cheap in most grocery stores, and pull it apart for this recipe. If you decide to go this route, taste the salad before adding salt and pepper, since rotisserie chickens are already seasoned.*

To cook chicken breasts yourself, preheat the oven to 400-degrees and put chicken breast on a baking sheet. Season with salt and pepper on both sides. Bake for 22 minutes or so, depending on the meat thickness, until the chicken has reached 165-degrees. Cool before making the salad.

Directions:

Shred chicken with clean hands and put in a bowl. Add chopped celery, Greek yogurt, and dried cranberries, if using. Mix well. Season with salt and pepper to taste.

Nutritional Info (½ recipe per serving):

Total calories: 304

Carbs: 6.8

Protein: 44.6

Fat: 10.9

Fiber: 0.9

Broiled Chicken Salad-Cheddar Sandwich

Serves: 1

Time: Around 5 minutes

If you have extra chicken salad left over from the recipe above, this is the perfect lunch or quick dinner to use it up. Just slap it between two slices of whole-grain bread (it has more protein and fiber than regular bread) with cheese and a few slices of tomato, and that's it!

Tip: *If you don't have time to make a hot sandwich, this is easily converted into a cold one. Leave off the mayo (the chicken salad is creamy enough on its own) and assemble sandwich as normal, adding a leaf of Romaine lettuce.*

Ingredients:

2 slices of bread (ideally whole-grain)

Spoonful of mayo

3 tablespoons chicken salad (look to recipe above)

1 slice of cheddar slice

2 slices of tomato

Directions:

Preheat the oven to broil. Spread mayo on the slices of bread and stick under the broiler for just 30 seconds or so, until bread is golden. All broilers are different, so don't wander far.

Spoon chicken salad on one of the pieces of bread and top with cheese. Stick under the broiler again. When cheese is sizzling, remove from the oven and top with tomato and other toasted bread slice. Enjoy!

Nutritional Info (1 recipe per serving):

Total calories: 338

Carbs: 24

Protein: 20

Fat: 18.6

Fiber: 2.4

Broiled Tomato-Mozzarella Sandwich (Vegetarian)

Serves: 1

Time: Around 5 minutes

It's amazing how delicious a simple tomato and mozzarella sandwich can be. This is inspired by an Italian caprese salad, which resembles that country's flag - white mozzarella, green basil, and red tomato. I replace fresh basil with dried basil, just for convenience. Broil the sandwich for just a few minutes, and you've got a delicious lunch.

Ingredients:

Drizzle of olive oil

2 slices of bread (ideally whole-grain)

2 slices of tomato

1 slice mozzarella cheese

Dried basil to taste

Tip: *In a pinch, you can skip the broiling and just make this sandwich a cold one, but it really isn't as good, so I recommend taking the few extra minutes to make it right. If you are making it cold, replace the olive oil with your favorite sandwich condiment (like mayo or hummus), since the oil is just there to help crisp up the bread under the broiler.*

Directions:

Preheat your oven to broil. When ready, drizzle sandwich slices with olive oil and stick under the broiler until the bread is golden. Remove from the oven, and add tomato, with mozzarella on top. Return to the broiler and let the cheese get melty and sizzly. Sprinkle on basil to taste and enjoy!

Nutritional Info (1 recipe per serving):

Total calories: 223

Carbs: 24.7

Protein: 15.2

Fat: 7.3

Fiber: 4.2

Turkey-Pesto Grilled Cheese

Serves: 1

Time: Around 10 minutes

This was one of my favorite hot sandwiches in college, because I adore pesto. The fresh flavor really gives this sandwich personality and it's so much better than just plain mayo. We're still using mayo in this recipe, but that's just to give the bread its crispiness. For cheese, I like provolone, because it melts really well and it's mild. Something stronger like cheddar fights with the pesto too much for my taste.

Note: *You're not actually eating the oil that goes on the pan, so we're not counting it in the ingredient list.*

Ingredients:

2 slices of bread (ideally whole-grain)

½ tablespoon of mayo

1 slice of provolone cheese

4 slices thin-sliced oven-roasted deli turkey

1 tablespoon pesto

Tip: *To make this sandwich vegetarian, replace the turkey with two tomato slices. This will significantly reduce the protein count.*

Directions:

Drizzle a little olive oil (or spray with non-stick spray) in a skillet or griddle and heat. While that's heating up, spread mayo on one side of both bread slices. When the skillet is ready, put the mayo side down, and top with cheese and turkey. Take the other piece of bread, and spread the side that doesn't have mayo with pesto. Put the pesto side down on the sandwich in the skillet.

Let the sandwich fry, until the side that's touching the skillet is golden. Flip and keep frying. Depending on the heat of your stovetop or griddle, it can take 10 minutes to finish the sandwich. Serve hot!

Nutritional Info (1 recipe per serving):

Total calories: 448

Carbs: 29

Protein: 39

Fat: 20

Fiber: 4.7

Turkey Sandwich (With Avocado and Hummus)

Serves: 1

Time: Less than 5 minutes

The classic turkey sandwich gets a bit of an upgrade with flavorful, creamy hummus and fresh avocado. I really like using hummus as a sandwich condiment because it adds so much flavor, and it's a fairly healthy alternative to mayo. Hummus has iron, folate, good fats, and more. It's also dairy-free, so if you're a vegan, just leave the turkey off the sammie and you're in the clear!

Ingredients:

2 slices of bread (ideally whole-grain)

1 tablespoon hummus

4 slices thin-sliced oven-roasted deli turkey

2 slices of avocado

2 slices tomato (optional)

Tip: *What can you do with the rest of the avocado? The easiest way to store it is to just wrap it tightly in plastic wrap or foil, and stick it in the fridge. While it should stay pretty green because of the lack of oxygen exposure, it's best to use it within the next two days or so. If you love avocado as much as I do, that shouldn't be a problem. If you find yourself at a loss about what to do with it or just not feeling a meal with avocado, hand it off to your friends. I'm sure there will be somebody more than eager to take it.*

Directions:

Toast your bread slices to your preferred color. Spread on hummus, then assemble sandwich with turkey, avocado, and tomato, if you like. Enjoy!

Nutritional Info (1 recipe with tomato per serving):

Total calories: 404

Carbs: 36

Protein: 34

Fat: 15

Fiber: 10

Cucumber-Tuna Sandwich

Serves: 1

Time: Less than 5 minutes

Ah yes, the classic tuna sammie. It seems basic, but it has served me well over the years. I like adding cucumber for a fresh crunch, and provolone, though really any kind of sliced cheese works. I also like to go easy on the mayo, but it's up to you. Do be sure to season really well with salt and pepper, or the sandwich will be pretty boring.

Ingredients:

One 3-ounce canned tuna

½ tablespoon mayo

2 slices of bread (ideally whole-grain)

1 slice of provolone

3 slices cucumber

Salt to taste

Black pepper to taste

Directions:

Open and drain the tuna. Scoop out half, saving the rest in a plastic baggie, in the fridge, for later. Mix tuna with mayo, salt, and pepper. Spoon on a slice of bread, then add slices of provolone and cucumber. Top with the other slice of bread and eat!

Nutritional Info (1 recipe per serving):

Total calories: 334

Carbs: 24

Protein: 31

Fat: 13

Fiber: 3.8

CHAPTER 7: POULTRY

Chicken is one of the most versatile meats out there. Thanks to its mild flavor, it's a great vehicle for all kinds of spices and preparations. In this section, you'll learn how to use chicken breasts and ground chicken sausage, as well as turkey (the other main poultry) for fast, easy meals. Remember, both chicken and turkey should be cooked to at least 165-degrees. Do try to avoid overcooking the meat, especially chicken breasts, or you'll end up with dry, throat-sticking dinners that are not appetizing. You want succulent, juicy chicken breasts and nicely-browned ground meat and sausage.

Note: For most of these recipes, cooking in the oven or on the stovetop makes the most sense, so there's quite a few without slow cooker or pressure cooker instructions.

Basic Chicken Breast or Thighs

Makes: 4 chicken breasts/4 chicken thighs

Time: About 25-40 minutes (depends on if you're making breasts or thighs)

To save time during the week, I'll often cook a few chicken breasts or thighs on a free Saturday or Sunday, and use the meat for the next few meals. Some of these recipes call for cooked chicken, and while you can make most of the recipes fairly quickly even if you cook the chicken right then, having some around already makes things even easier.

Properly stored, cooked chicken will last 3-4 days in the fridge, according to the USDA. Some people use it longer, but just for extra safety, I recommend going with what the experts say. You can freeze cooked chicken for up to 3 months; you just have to defrost it properly before use. Unless you have a big freezer, freezing cooked chicken probably isn't super convenient for you. Here's a recipe for basic chicken breast and thighs for use within 3-4 days:

Ingredients:

1 pound of chicken breast (about 4 breasts) _or_ 4 boneless chicken thighs

Water (for soaking)

Salt

Olive oil

Pepper

Directions:

To get really tender breast meat, I recommend soaking them in a mixture of water and some salt. Salt breaks down the fibers in the meat. Since thighs are naturally juicer, I haven't needed to soak. After about 15 minutes of the salt soak, rinse the breasts well and pat dry. If you're making thighs, just make sure they're dry, too, before putting a baking dish. Stick in the fridge for now.

Preheat the oven to 400-degrees. When the oven is hot, drizzle whatever chicken cut you're making with olive oil, and season on both sides with salt and pepper. For breasts, cook for 22-26 minutes, until the thickest part is 165-degrees. Depending on the thickness of the breasts, time will vary. If they are really fat, you can carefully slice them in half horizontally, so they cook faster. For thighs, bake for 20 minutes, then check the temperature.

In slow cooker:

Instead of putting chicken in the oven after soak, put in a slow cooker with ¼ cup of chicken stock, and cook on low for 3 hours. Check temperature before using or storing. For thighs, cook for 2-3 hours on high, or 4-5 hours on low.

In pressure cooker:

Put chicken or thighs in your pressure cooker and add ½ cup chicken stock. For breasts, set time to 7 minutes, then quick-release the pressure when time is up. For boneless thighs, set time to 8 minutes. Check the temperature. If the meat isn't quite at 165-degrees yet, you can finish cooking it on the "Sauté" setting. It's better to underestimate pressure cooking time than to go over; you can always cook food a little longer, but you can't fix overcooked meat.

Nutritional Info (1 (3-oz) breast/1 (3-oz) thigh):

Total calories: 102 / 188

Carbs: 0 / 0

Protein: 19 / 14

Fat: 2.2 / 14

Fiber: 0 / 0

Mexican Chicken + Rice

Serves: 2

Time: About 5 minutes

This extremely-fast dinner only takes about 5 minutes, and that's without the microwave! You're actually using microwavable rice (like Uncle Ben's), but you're cooking it in the skillet. Toss in some diced tomatoes, chicken, and salt, and you've got a hearty meal.

Ingredients:

1 package of microwavable flavored rice (like cilantro-lime Ready Rice from Uncle Ben's or Spanish-style Ready Rice)

2 tablespoons of chicken stock

2 cups diced tomatoes

2 cups cooked chicken

Salt to taste

Directions:

Pour rice into a skillet with 2 tablespoons of chicken stock. Heat and stir, until rice is hot. Add tomatoes, cooked chicken, and salt to taste. Serve hot!

Nutritional Info (½ recipe):

Total calories: 477

Carbs: 49.5

Protein: 48.4

Fat: 8.8

Fiber: 5

Creamy Basil Chicken + Rice

Serves: 2
Time: 35-40 minutes

This is one of my favorite comfort food meals; I make it at least once every two weeks. I like to use Jasmine rice, but Basmati should work just fine, too. You cook the rice and chicken at the same time - the rice on the stovetop and the chicken in the oven - and then mix them with cream, dried basil, salt, and pepper. You end up with a great cold-weather meal that sticks to your ribs. If you have cooked chicken already, all you have to do is cook the rice.

Tip: *If you don't have heavy cream, you can use half-and-half or Greek yogurt, though Greek yogurt will change the texture and taste of the meal a little bit - it's thicker and tangier, but still delicious.*

Ingredients:

1 cup Jasmine rice
2 cups water
1 large chicken breast
½ cup heavy cream
Dried basil to taste
Salt to taste
Black pepper to taste

Directions:

Mix the rice and water into a saucepan. Bring to a boil, stir, and reduce to low. Cover with a tight-fitting lid. Leave it alone for 15-20 minutes.

While that cooks, prepare the chicken. Season with salt and pepper, and stick in 400-degree oven for 12-15 minutes, until the thickest part is 165-degrees. Cut into bite-sized pieces.

When the rice time is up, remove the pot from the heat, keeping the lid on. Rest for 5 minutes or so, and then add chicken, cream, basil, salt, and pepper.

In slow cooker:

Combine rice and 2 cups of water in your slow cooker. Add a little salt. Put chicken on top and close the lid. Cook on high for 2-3 hours, or low for 4 hours.

Stir in heavy cream. Season well with basil, salt, and pepper.

In pressure cooker:

Pour rice and 1 ¾ cups of water into the pressure cooker and stir. Slice raw chicken and put on top of the rice. Do not stir. Seal the lid and adjust time to just 5 minutes. When time is up, wait for the pressure to come down naturally. When the pressure is gone, open up the pressure cooker and stir in heavy cream. Season well with basil, salt, and pepper.

Nutritional Info (½ recipe):

Total calories: 637
Carbs: 81
Protein: 23
Fat: 24
Fiber: 0

Chicken Enchilada Bake

Serves: 2

Time: 25 minutes

I love enchiladas; they're my go-to choice at Mexican places. This is a great recipe because it takes all the flavors of a chicken enchilada and makes it really easy. No need to roll tortillas, they're actually just cut up and layered in a baking dish with enchilada sauce, yogurt, meat, and cheese. It's sort of like a lasagna.

Ingredients:

1 cup shredded rotisserie chicken

¼ of a 28-oz can green enchilada sauce

¾ cup Greek yogurt

3 corn tortillas

1 cup shredded Mexican mix cheese

Directions:

Preheat the oven to 375-degrees. Cut the tortillas into little squares. Grease a small baking dish and layer with ½ of the chicken, ½ of the sauce, ½ of the yogurt, ½ of the tortillas, then ½ of the cheese. Layer again, using the rest of the ingredients. Cover with foil, and bake for 20 minutes or so. Uncover and bake another 5 minutes, until cheese is bubbling. Enjoy!

Nutritional Info (½ recipe):

Total calories: 306

Carbs: 25.3

Protein: 34.9

Fat: 7.6

Fiber: 3

Buffalo Chicken

Serves: 1

Time: 25-30 minutes

Buffalo wing sauce has a very distinct, savory flavor thanks to ingredients like garlic, hot sauce, and of course, butter. That butter is what gives wing sauce its silky-smooth texture. Just use your favorite brand in this recipe, which reminds me of chicken fingers at sports bars and watching football games at home.

Ingredients:

6 tablespoons all-purpose flour

1 tablespoon Italian seasoning

10 tablespoons panko bread crumbs

¼ cup Buffalo wing sauce

1 large chicken breast

Directions:

Preheat oven to 400-degrees.In a bowl, mix flour and Italian seasoning. In a second bowl, add bread crumbs, and then in a third, the wing sauce.

Take the chicken and coat in flour/Italian seasoning, then dip in wing sauce, and lastly breadcrumbs. Pat gently with your fingers to completely coat the chicken and make the crumbs stick. Lay in a baking dish.

Bake in the oven for 15-20 minutes, until the thickest part of the chicken is at least 165-degrees. Serve!

Nutritional Info (1 recipe per serving):

Total calories: 437

Carbs: 63

Protein: 30

Fat: 4.5

Fiber: 2

Baked Chicken Provolone

Serves: 1

Time: Around 15 minutes

Chicken and cheese is a combo that's hard to beat. In this recipe, you're going to use both the stovetop and the broiler to get a cheesy, juicy dinner that's great on its own or with a salad on the side. You just season the chicken breast, cook in a skillet, and then stick under the broiler with a piece of ham and cheese on top. It only takes a few minutes to melt the cheese and get the ham a little crispy.

Ingredients:

Splash of olive oil

1 large chicken breast

Black pepper to taste

Dried basil to taste

1 slice of deli ham

1 slice provolone cheese

Directions:

Heat oil in a skillet until hot and shiny. Season both sides of the chicken with pepper, and cook in the hot skillet for 4-5 minutes per side, until the thickest part of the chicken is 165-degrees.

Turn on the oven broiler. Move chicken to a baking sheet, seasoning with basil. Lay ham and cheese on top. Broil until cheese is melted, which should be just 1-2 minutes. Serve!

Nutritional Info (1 recipe per serving):

Total calories: 297

Carbs: 1.7

Protein: 41

Fat: 13

Fiber: 0

Turkey Sloppy Joes

Serves: 1

Time: 10-15 minutes

When I'm in a rush and the kids need to eat, honestly, Sloppy Joes are my go-to. It's extremely easy, quick, and fills up hungry bellies. It fills up hungry college students, too, and you only need 10-15 minutes to make this meal from scratch. That classic Sloppy Joe flavor is just ketchup, mustard, brown sugar, and a little salt. Mix with cooked ground meat and slap between a hamburger bun.

Tip: *You can substitute ground beef for the turkey, if you have it.*

Ingredients:

¼ pound ground turkey

1 ½ tablespoons ketchup

½ tablespoon mustard

½ tablespoon brown sugar

Salt to taste

1 hamburger bun

Directions:

Brown turkey in a skillet. If it looks like it's getting dry and stuck, just splash in a little water. When brown, drain any excess juice.

Mix ketchup, mustard, and brown sugar into the meat. You can just add it right to the skillet; no need to mix the sauce in a separate bowl. Taste and season with salt if needed. Simmer on low for a few minutes to blend the flavors.

Serve on hamburger buns.

Nutritional Info (1 sloppy joe per serving):

Total calories: 357

Carbs: 37

Protein: 23

Fat: 11

Fiber: 1.3

Chicken Sausage Bake

Serves: 2

Time: 20-25 minutes

On cold nights, I love pasta bakes. They warm up the body and soul, and are so easy to put together in less than a half hour. This recipe is really easy to double, too, if you want. The only hands-on cooking is browning the ground chicken sausage in oil, while the pasta boils. You can use the same skillet you cooked the sausage in, and just add sauce, cooked pasta, and top with cheese. Bake until the cheese is bubbly and starting to get a little brown.

Ingredients:

Water (for boiling)

8 ounces penne pasta (about ½ of a box)

½ tablespoon olive oil

½ pound ground chicken sausage

1 ½ cups marinara sauce

1 cup shredded mozzarella cheese

Salt to taste

Directions:

Fill a pot with water and bring to a boil. Add penne pasta and cook for 7 minutes or so, until the pasta is al dente. While that's cooking, heat oil in an oven-safe skillet and cook the chicken sausage. Now is a good time to preheat the oven, too, to 350-degrees.

When sausage is cooked through, pour sauce in skillet and simmer for a little bit. When pasta is done, drain. Pour in the skillet with the chicken and sauce, and stir. Taste and season with salt if needed. Sprinkle on cheese. Stick skillet in the oven for 10-12 minutes, until the cheesy is hot and bubbly.

Tip: *If you're in a rush, you can just dump the cooked sausage and sauce, pasta, and cheese in a bowl, and stir. No baking necessary.*

Nutritional Info (½ recipe):

Total calories: 756

Carbs: 88.4

Protein: 40.2

Fat: 25.7

Fiber: 4.9

Chicken Sausage Fajitas

Serves: 1-2

Time: About 15 minutes

In college, I really depended on precooked chicken sausage for fast meals. They're healthier than hot dogs, and there are a variety of flavors like sweet apple sausages and spicier Italian-inspired ones. You can eat them like you would a normal hot dog, cut them up into pasta, or turn them in these fast sheet-pan fajitas. Just toss with some bell peppers and taco seasoning, bake to blend the flavors and heat up the meat, and serve on flour tortillas with iceberg lettuce.

Ingredients:

2 precooked chicken sausages

1 bell pepper

Taco seasoning to taste

2 flour tortillas

Handful of iceberg lettuce

Directions:

Preheat oven to 400-degrees. Slice your chicken sausages into coins, and slice the bell pepper. Put in a bowl and toss with taco seasoning. Put spiced sausage/peppers on a parchment-lined baking sheet and bake for about 15 minutes. Serve on tortillas with iceberg lettuce.

Nutritional Info (1 recipe):

Total calories: 509

Carbs: 44.9

Protein: 26.9

Fat: 25.7

Fiber: 4.8

CHAPTER 8: BEEF & PORK

When chicken gets boring, nothing hits the spot like beef or pork. Flavor and protein-packed, both meats hold up to a variety of spices. In this section, you'll find recipes for hot dogs that skip the normal ketchup-and-mustard routine for something more interesting, as well as fast and nutritious dinners like a breakfast-inspired pork burger, vegetable + beef ramen, and pork fried rice. For those wanting to stretch their cooking skills a bit and impress people (even a special someone), there's steak dinner for two recipe and pork roast eager to be served at a dinner party.

Breakfast-for-Dinner Pork Burger

Serves: 1

Time: Around 12-15 minutes

Hamburgers are one of my favorite foods on earth, but when I was in college, I didn't have all the spices necessary to make a really good patty. So, I started experimenting with ground sausage, which already has seasonings, and found that I really liked ground pork sausage burgers with an egg on top. To add some smokiness, paprika was all that was needed. Cook in a skillet, use that same skillet to fry an egg, and that's it!

Ingredients:

¼ pound ground pork breakfast sausage

Sprinkle of paprika

1 egg

1 hamburger bun

Salt to taste

Cooking spray

Directions:

Get out the ground breakfast sausage and sprinkle with paprika. Massage spice into the meat with your hands, so it's as evenly-mixed as possible. Form meat into patty. Heat skillet on medium, testing with a drop of water. It will sizzle when hot enough. Coat with cooking spray and add patty. Sear until nicely-browned on one side, then flip and sear that other side. Check temperature; you want at least 160-degrees for pork sausage. If the meat isn't quite done, but the outside is seared to your preferred color, turn down the burner, so the outside doesn't burn.

When done, plate patty and cover to keep warm. In the still-hot skillet, crack an egg. Season the top with salt and fry, so the whites are solid, but the yolk isn't hard. Put the patty on your hamburger bun and top with fried egg. Serve!

Nutritional Info (1 breakfast burger):

Total calories: 567

Carbs: 21.6

Protein: 31.7

Fat: 38.4

Fiber: 0.9

Hot Dogs with Peach Salsa

Serves: 1-2

Time: Less than 10 minutes

Hot dogs may not be the healthiest meat out there, but they are tasty and really easy. You can also find better hot dogs for a decent price, which was tricky when I was in college. I really like Applegate organic uncured beef hot dogs and Hebrew National's, a classic dog. Instead of just simple ketchup and mustard, the hot dog gets elevated with a really simple peach salsa. You'll never want to eat hot dogs any other way!

Ingredients:

1 ripe peach

1 fresh jalapeno (if you don't want the heat, sub with jarred banana peppers)

Squirt of lime juice

Water (for cooking hot dogs)

Two hot dogs

Two hot dog buns

Tip: *When cutting hot peppers, I really recommend wearing polyethylene gloves. The oils make your hands burn otherwise. If you forget, just plan on washing your hands right after with dish (not hand) soap. If your hands start burning, try home remedies like dunking them in yogurt, cold milk, or ice water.*

Directions:

Let's make the salsa first. Carefully cut the peach in half, and remove the pit. Chop into small pieces and put in a bowl. Ideally, you want gloves to cut the jalapenos. Cut the jalapeno, removing the seeds with a spoon, and cut into small pieces. Toss with peaches. Squirt the salsa with lime juice and place in the fridge for now.

Time to cook your hot dogs. Pour water into a skillet, just so ½-inch is covered. Turn heat to medium and wait until the water starts to boil and evaporate. Add hot dogs and cook, rolling it around occasionally, until it starts to brown.

Put hot dogs in buns and top with salsa. Serve!

Avocado salsa variation:

1 small avocado

2 tablespoons chopped red onion (or more to your taste)

Lime juice

Pineapple salsa variation:

¾ cup canned pineapple

2 tablespoons chopped red onion (or more to your taste)

Nutritional Info (1 hot dog + ½ salsa recipe):

Total calories: 152

Carbs: 20.4

Protein: 6.3

Fat: 4.7

Fiber: 1.4

Vegetable + Beef Ramen

Serves: 2

Time: Around 15 minutes

A lot of people I knew lived on ramen noodles, and most of them didn't really try anything interesting with them. However, the noodles and seasoning packet are really just the beginning. You can add all kinds of nutritious and tasty vegetables, and a protein, like ground beef. That's what I did in this recipe, and used the seasoning packet to season the beef. For even more flavor, cook noodles in chicken stock instead of plain water.

Ingredients:

½ pound ground beef

1 package ramen noodles (keep seasoning packet)

2 ½ cups chicken stock

2 cups frozen mixed vegetables

Dash of sriracha (optional)

Directions:

Heat skillet and add ground beef. Because beef is fatty, you don't need oil, though if it starts to look dry, add a little chicken stock. Once browned, stir in the ramen noodle seasoning packet.

In a pot, add stock, noodles, and frozen vegetables. Bring to a boil, and then reduce heat. Cover with lid and simmer until noodles and veggies are tender. It should only take 3 minutes or so.

Mix beef and ramen in a bowl. If you like a little heat, add sriracha. Enjoy!

Nutritional Info (½ recipe):

Total calories: 436

Carbs: 37.7

Protein: 43

Fat: 11.5

Fiber: 9

Cheesy-Beef Noodles

Serves: 2

Time: Around 15-20 minutes

This was my "I had a bad day" meal back in college. It wasn't the healthiest dinner in the world, but it was satisfying to my soul. Beef, noodles, sauce, and cheese. It's basically spaghetti, which always reminds me of home. If you're watching your red meat consumption, swap out ground beef for ground turkey or chicken.

Ingredients:

¼ pound beef

½ pound elbow macaroni noodles

1 ½ cups marinara sauce

1 cup shredded cheddar cheese

Italian seasoning to taste

Water (for boiling)

Salt to taste

Black pepper to taste

Directions:

Heat a skillet on medium and add beef, stirring every once and a while, until the meat is brown. While that cooks, fill a pot with 4 cups of water and toss in some salt. Turn heat to high and bring to a boil. Add elbow macaroni noodles and cook according to the package instructions. This should take about 9 minutes. The meat should be done by now. Pour in sauce and reduce heat to low. The sauce will simmer the beef, creating a richer flavor.

Drain noodles. Pour beef and sauce mixture into the pasta. Stir. Add cheese, stirring again to melt. Add Italian seasoning, salt, and pepper to taste. Serve hot!

Nutritional Info (½ recipe):

Total calories: 886

Carbs: 111

Protein: 43

Fat: 28

Fiber: 8.5

Date Night Steak with Garlic-Butter Broccoli

Serves: 2

Time: Around 15 minutes

I know steak isn't cheap. That's why this is a "date night" recipe, or a recipe you splurge on in order to impress a certain somebody. Still, keeping budget in mind, go with a cheaper cut. I like boneless flank steak because it's fairly easy to cook in addition to being affordable. You sear it in a really hot skillet and then stick in the oven to finish cooking, with butter on top. Prepare some frozen broccoli, add butter and seasonings, and you've got a great dinner for two!

Ingredients:

Two boneless flank steaks

3 tablespoons butter

3 cups frozen broccoli

Garlic powder (to taste)

Salt (to taste)

Pepper (to taste)

Cooking spray

Directions:

Preheat the oven to 400-degrees. You will finish the steaks there. Remove steak from the fridge and sprinkle each side generously with salt and pepper. Heat a large skillet (big enough to fit both steaks) on high. To see if the skillet is hot enough, flick in a drop of water. It should sizzle. Spray with cooking spray and lay in steaks. Sear on high for just 2-3 minutes, then flip. After another 2-3 minutes, top with 2 tablespoons of butter and move steak to oven.

Cook for just 3 minutes and check the temperature. You want at least 130-140 degrees, which is rare, heading to medium-rare. Plate steak and tent with foil to keep warm. It will continue to cook, which is why it's very important not to overcook the steak in the oven.

Prepare the broccoli. Mix in 1 tablespoon of butter, salt, pepper, and garlic powder to taste. Serve!

Nutritional Info (4-ounces steak + 1 ½ cups broccoli):

Total calories: 419

Carbs: 9.1

Protein: 35.6

Fat: 27.2

Fiber: 3.6

Dinner Party Pork Roast

Serves: 4

Time: 1 hour, 20 minutes

While not the fastest recipe in this book, this pork tenderloin roast is perfect for students (or anyone, really) who wants to cook something special for a gathering. This might include a dinner party for students who can't get home for the holidays. There's very few ingredients needed and all you really need to do is brown the pork, and then keep an eye on it in the oven. No fancy techniques here.

Tip: *Pork gets dry very quickly and most people tend to overcook it. You do want at least 145-degrees for safety, but as you get higher than that, the drier the pork gets. Don't let your eyeballs scare you: a little pink in your pork is okay, as long as the thermometer reads at least 145-degrees.*

Ingredients:

2 pounds pork tenderloin roast
Dried garlic to taste
2 tablespoons olive oil
4 tablespoons butter
1 tablespoon Italian seasoning
Salt to taste
Black pepper to taste

Directions:

Preheat your oven to 350-degrees. Remove the pork from the fridge and season generously with garlic, salt, and pepper.

Get a large skillet (that can go in the oven and is big enough for the roast) and heat olive oil, until shiny and starting to sizzle. Sear the pork on all sides, which should take just 1 minute per side or so. When nicely-browned, put the pork on a plate for now.

Add butter to the skillet and melt. Sprinkle in Italian seasoning. Put the pork back into the skillet and spoon over the melted butter/herb mixture.

Cover skillet with foil, so pork loin is covered, and roast in the preheated oven for a half hour. Using foil helps keep the juices contained. When that time is up, take off the foil. Spoon more of the melted butter over the pork, so it doesn't dry out, and return to the oven with foil covering for 30 minutes. You want the temperature to be at least 145-degrees.

When that temp is reached, carefully remove the pork loin and plate. Tent with foil and wait 15 minutes. Now, it's ready to slice and serve!

Nutritional Info (¼ pork tenderloin):

Total calories: 403
Carbs: 0
Protein: 48.3
Fat: 23.5
Fiber: 0

Pork Fried Rice

Serves: 2

Time: About 15 minutes

This recipe is easiest when you have leftover white rice. You can make it with fresh rice, but it takes longer, and honestly, it doesn't taste quite as good. Cook sausage first in olive oil, then cook scrambled eggs in the same saucepan. Using the same pan for a third time, cook veggies, and then mix everything together.

Ingredients:

2 tablespoons olive oil

½ pound ground pork sausage

2 eggs

1 cup frozen veggies

1 ½ cups cooked rice

Salt to taste

Black pepper to taste

Directions:

Heat 1 tablespoon of oil until hot and shiny. Add ground pork sausage and cook to at least 160-degrees. Plate.

In a bowl, whisk eggs with salt and pepper. Using the fat from the pork, cook eggs. Plate.

Scrap the saucepan, so any stuck bits of egg don't burn. Add more oil and heat. Add frozen veggies and stir to heat through. Add rice, eggs, and pork sausage. Stir until everything is hot. Serve!

Nutritional Info (½ recipe):

Total calories: 744

Carbs: 44.3

Protein: 30.1

Fat: 48.8

Fiber: 1.7

Korean Beef Bowl with Zucchini Coins

Serves: 2

Time: Around 15 minutes

This easy beef and rice bowl takes flavors from Asia thanks to sweet chili sauce. For veggies, I really love zucchini, which manages to be both fresh and buttery at the same time. Cook zucchini in the skillet you cooked the beef in, and then mix everything with rice. Green onions are optional, but nice. They add a nice burst of acid.

Ingredients:

½ pound ground beef

¼ cup sweet chili sauce

1 zucchini

1 ½ cups cooked white rice

Green onions (optional)

Salt to taste

Ingredients:

Heat a skillet and cook ground beef. When brown and at least 160-degrees, turn heat to low and mix in sweet chili sauce. Let that simmer.

Cut the zucchini into coins. When sliced, remove ground beef from skillet, and sauté the coins in the leftover beef fat, until softened and beginning to brown.

Tip: *If you want to cook rice specifically for this recipe, here's a reminder on how to do it - Bring 2 cups of water and 1 cup of rice to a boil. Reduce heat to low/medium. Cover with a lid and simmer for 15-20 minutes. Rice will absorb water.*

Return beef to skillet, along with cooked white rice, and stir. When everything is heated through, taste, and salt as needed. Serve with sliced green onions, if you have some on hand.

Taco beef bowl variation:

Sub sweet chili sauce with a generous sprinkle of taco seasoning. Skip the zucchini and green onion, and instead top with raw chopped tomato and avocado.

Nutritional Info (½ recipe):

Total calories: 406

Carbs: 55.2

Protein: 27

Fat: 6.3

Fiber: 1.5

CHAPTER 9: SEAFOOD

You might think seafood is out of the question on a college student's budget, but by making smart choices, you can enjoy shrimp and fish on a regular basis. I liked to buy a bag of precooked shrimp, for convenience sake, and plenty of canned tuna. I also kept my eye on sales for when affordable white fish (like tilapia) got even cheaper. Frozen fillets are always nice to have around. Seafood is full of nutrients like vitamin B, protein, good cholesterol, and more. While you may not be able to afford enough seafood to eat it twice a week (which is what health experts recommend), these recipes do let you make it more often.

Shrimp Alfredo Pasta

Serves: 1

Time: About 20 minutes

One of my favorite pasta dishes is shrimp Alfredo. It's rich and creamy and perfect for cold winter nights. This recipe is easy to double, triple, or quadrouble for more servings if you're feeding more than yourself, or want enough for leftovers. Because of the creaminess of the dish, it tends to get a bit weird heated up in the microwave, so I don't recommend keeping it around longer than 3 days or so.

Ingredients:

¼ of a 16-ounce box of uncooked penne pasta
¼ pound cooked shrimp
1 cup frozen broccoli
½ cup Alfredo sauce from a jar
Handful of Parmesan cheese
Salt (to taste)
Water (for boiling)

Tip: *If you don't like broccoli, substitute with frozen peas.*

Directions:

Cook pasta according to directions on the box. While pasta is cooking, take out frozen shrimp and broccoli, and put in a colander. Run under hot water until close to thawed. Pat dry with paper towels and set aside for now. When pasta is al dente, drain. Mix in broccoli and shrimp. When both are heated through, stir in Alfredo sauce and top with cheese. Taste and salt if necessary.

Nutritional Info (1 recipe per serving):

Total calories: 652
Carbs: 72.8
Protein: 52.2
Fat: 16.8
Fiber: 2.4

Sesame Shrimp

Serves: 1

Time: Less than 10 minutes (with cooked rice)

All this recipe needs for maximum flavor is a sesame salad dressing and Italian seasoning. Precooked shrimp gets thawed quickly under hot water, and then simmers for a minute or so in the dressing. Kraft makes a cheap sesame salad dressing, as does Newman's Own, if you want something a little nicer. Serve over rice or noodles. If you use leftover cooked rice, the recipe takes less than 10 minutes. If you cook rice, it adds 20 minutes or so.

Ingredients:

¼ pound cooked frozen shrimp

2 tablespoons sesame salad dressing

Italian seasoning to taste

1 cup cooked white rice (to serve)

Salt to taste

Directions:

Put frozen shrimp in a colander and run under hot water until thawed. In a skillet, heat 1 tablespoon of salad dressing. Add shrimp and stir, cooking for a minute or so. Add in the rest of the dressing and Italian seasoning. Taste and salt if necessary. Serve with rice! It's also great with egg noodles or ramen.

Tip: *To cook rice, use 2 cups of water for every 1 cup of uncooked rice. Bring water and rice to a boil. Reduce to a simmer and cover with a lid. Cook for 15-20 minutes or so, until the rice has absorbed the water and is fluffy.*

Nutritional Info (1 recipe per serving):

Total calories: 509

Carbs: 57.7

Protein: 31.2

Fat: 15.8

Fiber: 0.3

Garlic Butter Shrimp 'n Rice

Serves: 1

Time: Less than 10 minutes (with cooked rice)

Shrimp is so naturally succulent on its own, it doesn't need much in way of flavorings and seasonings. In this recipe, we're using garlic - either fresh or dried - to make a buttery garlic sauce. This mixes with cooked shrimp, rice, and some parmesan cheese. It's basically shrimp scampi with rice instead of pasta.

Ingredients:

¼ pound cooked frozen shrimp

2 tablespoons butter

Dried garlic to taste (or two chopped cloves fresh garlic)

1 cup cooked rice

Handful of parmesan cheese

Salt to taste

Directions:

To thaw shrimp, put in a colander and run under warm water. Melt butter in a skillet. If you're using fresh garlic, add now, and stir for 3 minutes or so. Don't leave the skillet or the garlic might burn. Add shrimp and cook for a minute or so. If you're using dried garlic, add now.

Add rice to the skillet and mix. Top with cheese. Taste and add salt if needed.

Tip: *To cook rice for this recipe, bring 2 cups of water and 1 cup of rice to a boil. Reduce heat to low/medium. Cover with a lid and simmer for 15-20 minutes. Rice will absorb water.*

Nutritional Info (1 recipe per serving):

Total calories: 670

Carbs: 56.2

Protein: 39.4

Fat: 31.3

Fiber: 0

Easy Fish Tacos

Serves: 2

Time: Around 10-12 minutes

I always think of summers at the beach when I eat fish tacos. In this recipe, I keep things really simple by cooking white fish fillets rubbed with taco seasoning in oil, and then wrapping pieces up in a tortilla with some store-bought coleslaw. Hit with a little salt if needed. Remember: fish cooks way faster than other meat, so stay near the skillet and keep your thermometer close. You don't want overcooked fish.

Ingredients:

2 white fish fillets

2 tablespoons taco seasoning

2 tablespoons olive oil

1 cup store-bought coleslaw

2 corn tortillas

Salt to taste

Directions:

Season fish with taco seasoning. Heat oil in a skillet. When hot, cook fish fillets about 3-5 minutes per side, until 145-degrees. Rest 5 minutes.

To assemble tacos, divide fish and coleslaw among two tortillas. Serve!

Nutritional Info (1 recipe per serving):

Total calories: 456

Carbs: 40.4

Protein: 36.9

Fat: 16.4

Fiber: 3.3

Salmon Patty

Serves: 1

Time: 6-7 minutes

I don't think I really thought about canned salmon until I looked up recipes for salmon patties. I had enjoyed a salmon patty sandwich at a restaurant, and wanted to see how difficult they were to make at home. Answer: they're not difficult at all! Just use a little can of salmon (you can find them with canned tuna), a bit of egg, onion, breadcrumbs, salt, and pepper. Fry in a skillet, like you would cook a hamburger, and enjoy!

Ingredients:

One 5-ounce can of salmon

½ egg

2 ½ teaspoons chopped onion

1 ½ tablespoons dry bread crumbs

½ teaspoon olive oil

Salt to taste

Black pepper to taste

Tip: *To measure ½ cup egg, beat in a bowl and measure out 2 tablespoons.*

Directions:

Drain salmon, keeping the liquid. Mix salmon, egg, onion, and dry bread crumbs. Season well with salt and pepper. Mold into patty with your hands. If the mixture is too dry and not sticking together, add salmon liquid.

Heat olive oil in a skillet until shiny and hot. Put patty in the skillet and brown on each side. Canned salmon is already cooked, so don't worry about undercooked fish. Serve with rice, a salad, or a bun.

Nutritional Info (1 recipe per serving):

Total calories: 332

Carbs: 5

Protein: 37

Fat: 20

Fiber: 0

Tuna Zucchini Boats

Serves: 1

Time: 25-30 minutes

A great option for anyone trying to cut out carbs from their diet, these tuna zucchini boats are flavorful and nutritious. You actually cook the zucchini you scoop out of the "shells," so nothing is wasted. The insides are cooked in oil with red onion, tuna, salt, and pepper, and then baked in the zucchini hollows. It's like a tuna melt, but with a vegetable "bread."

Ingredients:

1 medium zucchini

Splash of olive oil

¼ cup diced red onion

One 5-ounce can of tuna

¼ cup shredded cheese

Salt to taste

Black pepper to taste

Directions:

Preheat oven to 400-degrees. Cut zucchini in half and scoop out as much of the inside as you can. Dice up the zucchini innards. Heat oil in a skillet until hot. Sauté zucchini dices and red onion until softened.

Add tuna and stir for just a minute or so. Salt and pepper well. Spoon mixture into zucchini hollows and sprinkle on cheese. Bake in oven for 15-20 minutes, until the cheese is melted.

Nutritional Info (1 recipe per serving):

Total calories: 411

Carbs: 7

Protein: 46

Fat: 21

Fiber: 2

Cheesy Tuna Potato Hash

Serves: 1

Time: 15 minutes

For a very easy dinner hash, replace the usual eggs with tuna. All the other essentials are there, i.e. breakfast potatoes and cheese. Fry the potatoes in oil, so they're nicely browned and getting crispy, and then cook with a can of tuna. It all comes together with salt, pepper, and cheddar cheese.

Ingredients:

1 tablespoon olive oil

1 cup of frozen breakfast potatoes

One 5-oz can of tuna

¼ cup of shredded cheddar cheese

Salt to taste

Black pepper to taste

Directions:

Heat oil in a skillet. Add frozen breakfast potatoes in a single layer, breaking up any frozen chunks with a wooden spoon. Fry, stirring occasionally, for 10 minutes or so until browned and tender.

Drain tuna and stir into the potatoes. Add cheese, stirring to melt, and season well with salt and pepper.

Nutritional Info (1 recipe per serving):

Total calories: 639

Carbs: 33

Protein: 48

Fat: 35

Fiber: 2.2

Lemon-Garlic Fish with Roasted Broccoli

Serves: 1

Time: Around 15 minutes

I love figuring out 5-ingredient recipes that include both a main dish and a side. It makes me feel like a kitchen wizard. In this meal, you roast frozen broccoli with oil, salt, and pepper in a very hot oven, and as that gets close to being done, you quickly fry up a white fish fillet seasoned with garlic, salt, and pepper. The whole plate gets a healthy squeeze of fresh lemon juice, and you've got a super healthy and tasty dinner!

Ingredients:

3 tablespoons olive oil

1 cup frozen broccoli

One white fish fillet

Dried garlic to taste

½ lemon

Salt to taste

Black pepper to taste

Directions:

Preheat a 450-degree oven. Once that's hot, prepare broccoli by breaking it up into florets, if necessary. Spread on a baking sheet and toss with 2 tablespoons of olive oil. Season with salt and pepper. Roast for 12-15 minutes until tender.

When the broccoli has about 5 minutes left, season fish with dried garlic, salt, and pepper. Put 1 tablespoon of oil into a skillet and heat. When hot, cook fish for 2 minutes, then flip. Cook until fish is at least 145-degrees. Serve with broccoli. Squeeze half a lemon over the fish and veggies. Enjoy!

Nutritional Info (1 recipe per serving):

Total calories: 524

Carbs: 6

Protein: 27

Fat: 44

Fiber: 2.4

Tilapia with Herb-Seasoned Yogurt

Serves: 1

Time: Less than 10 minutes

Fish and dairy sometimes get a bad rap, but they can actually go really well together. The dairy in this recipe is yogurt freshened up with Italian seasoning and brightened with lemon juice. It makes a really awesome sauce for broiled tilapia.

Ingredients:

One tilapia fillet

4 tablespoons plain Greek yogurt

½ tablespoon Italian seasoning

Squirt of lemon juice

Salt to taste

Black pepper to taste

Cooking spray (for cookie sheet)

Directions:

Move rack in oven to the very top. Preheat oven to broil. Season tilapia with salt and pepper, and spray a cookie sheet. Lay fish on sheet.

Broil fish for 5 minutes. While that cooks, mix Greek yogurt, Italian seasoning, and lemon juice in a bowl. Check fish - it should be at least 145-degrees.

Spread yogurt sauce on fish and enjoy! If you want a side, serve with a green salad, roasted veggies, or rice.

Nutritional Info (1 recipe per serving):

Total calories: 212

Carbs: 6.1

Protein: 41

Fat: 2.6

Fiber: 0

CHAPTER 10: SOUPS & STEWS

For an easy lunch or dinner, I often turn to soup or stew. These one-pot meals are perfect vehicles for all kinds of healthy ingredients and spices, and they can often be stored for quite a while in the fridge or frozen! It's easy to make soups and stews in larger portions, so all these recipes are portioned for 4 people, or, what's more likely, one person for about 4 days. That's how long most of these soups will last in the fridge, in the right container. If you don't think you will want to eat the same soup for 4 days, just half the recipe.

Tips on equipment:

For soups and stews, I really like using a slow cooker or the pressure cooking setting on a multi-cooker, but I understand that those appliances might not be available or convenient to a college student. For that reason, the recipes are designed for stovetop stock pots. I've included instructions on how to make them in a slow cooker or pressure cooker, as well, if you have one. If the soup is really quick on the stovetop and doesn't require much active time, it doesn't really make sense to have a slow cooker or pressure cooker version, so I've left those recipes as is.

A few of these soups are pureed, so I really recommend having either a blender, food processor, or immersion blender.

Classic Creamy Tomato Soup (Vegetarian)

Serves: 4 (or 1 person for 4 days)

Time: Around 6-7 minutes

I believe everyone should know how to make tomato soup from scratch. It's one of the easiest meals to throw together and bursting with flavor. I like using canned diced tomatoes for convenience, but if you do want to use fresh, I highly-recommend getting them at a farmer's market. Regular tomatoes from the grocery store just aren't as good. Roast them for 40 minutes at 400-degrees (better flavor) before making the soup.

Tip: *If you can swing it, budget-wise, I recommend replacing dried basil with fresh leaves. The taste of fresh basil really upgrades this simple soup.*

Ingredients:

Two 15-ounce cans of diced tomatoes

Dried basil to taste (or fresh basil)

Garlic powder to taste

½ cup heavy cream

Salt to taste

Black pepper to taste

Directions:

If you have a blender or food processor, blend the tomatoes and spices together. You can also use an immersion blender to get the tomatoes pureed.

Pour blended spiced tomato mixture into a saucepan and turn the burner to medium-low. Pour in cream, letting the soup slowly heat up while you stir. It should take just 5 minutes or so to get to the right temperature. Enjoy! Refrigerate leftovers no longer than 4 days.

Nutritional Info (¼ recipe per serving):

Total calories: 169

Carbs: 16

Protein: 4.3

Fat: 11

Fiber: 4

Chicken Wild Rice Soup

Serves: 4 (or 1 person for 4 days)

Time: Less than 10 minutes

On winter days, my mom always made chicken wild rice soup, and my first year in college, I really started missing it. I got the kind in a can, but it just wasn't the same. This stripped-down version uses microwaved wild rice from a brand like Uncle Ben's, rotisserie or leftover chicken, chicken stock, condensed cream of mushroom soup, and dried basil.

Tip: *You'll notice this recipe doesn't include salt. That's because the cream of mushroom soup has both salt and garlic in it. If you taste the soup and find it lacking in flavor, feel free to add salt of your own. You could also buy a chicken broth with salt (like Swanson's Chicken Cooking Stock) to ensure a more flavorful soup, though you have less control over the sodium content that way.*

Ingredients:

6-ounces raw wild rice (like Uncle Ben's)

4 cups unsalted chicken broth

2 cups cooked chicken (from a previous meal or a rotisserie chicken)

1 cup condensed cream of mushroom soup

Dried basil to taste

Directions:

Prepare rice according to instructions. Pour chicken broth into a pot and bring to a boil over medium-high heat. Add the cooked rice and simmer for just 5 minutes or so. Add the rest of the ingredients and cook for another couple of minutes, until the soup is hot. Serve! Keep leftovers in the fridge no longer than 4 days.

Nutritional Info (¼ recipe per serving):

Total calories: 326

Carbs: 37.1

Protein: 29.6

Fat: 6.3

Fiber: 2.6

Chilled Cucumber Soup

Serves: 1

Time: About 20 minutes

While chilled chicken noodle soup or chili wouldn't be very good, there are soups designed to be served cold. They are common in hot climates and perfect for summer nights when you want a meal that's really fast and refreshing. This soup combines cucumbers, Greek yogurt, lemon juice, Italian seasoning, salt, and pepper for a smooth, bright mouthful that's great as a light meal or side to a bigger dish.

Ingredients:

2 chopped cucumbers

1 ½ cups plain Greek yogurt

1 tablespoon lemon juice

Italian seasoning to taste

Salt to taste

Black pepper to taste

Directions:

Blend cucumbers, yogurt, and lemon juice in your blender. When smooth, add Italian seasoning, salt, and pepper. Taste and adjust seasonings as needed. Chill in the fridge until very cold.

Nutritional Info (1 recipe per serving):

Total calories: 349

Carbs: 39

Protein: 38

Fat: 7.3

Fiber: 3.1

Turkey + White Bean Soup (With Spinach)

Serves: 4 (or 1 person for 4 days)
Time: 25-30 minutes

Nutritious and low in calories, this soup is great if you're trying to eat healthier without sacrificing good flavors. Turkey and white beans are full of protein, while spinach adds essential nutrients like potassium and iron. Both of those minerals are known for their energizing effects, which is so important during busy college days.

Tip: *To change up this soup, you can substitute quite a few ingredients, like ground chicken or ground beef for the turkey; kale or arugula for the spinach; and black beans or cooked lentils for the white beans.*

Ingredients:

1 tablespoon olive oil
¼ pound ground turkey
6 cups chicken stock
Two 15-ounce cans of white beans
Generous handful of spinach
Salt to taste
Black pepper to taste

Directions:

Add oil to a skillet and heat until shiny. Cook the ground turkey until browned, and drain the juice. Season well with salt and pepper.

Pour stock into a stockpot, and add the cooked turkey, and drained beans. Bring to a boil on medium-high, then reduce to a simmer for 5 minutes or so. Stir in spinach (it will wilt pretty quickly), and salt to taste. Serve! Leftovers should keep about 4 days in the fridge.

In slow cooker:

Brown the meat as normal. You can technically cook raw ground meat in a slow cooker, but I highly recommend against it for food safety reasons. Put browned turkey, beans, and chicken stock in your slow cooker. Cook on low for 4 hours. Stir in spinach and season before serving.

In pressure cooker:

Cook ground meat in your pressure cooker, lid off, on the "Sauté" setting. When that's cooked, add stock and beans. Seal the lid and pressure cook for 2 minutes. When the pressure cooker beeps, wait 10 minutes or so before venting. Beans are a starchy food, so opening the valve too soon can cause foaming. Add spinach, salt, and pepper.

Nutritional Info (¼ recipe per serving):

Total calories: 289
Carbs: 46.5
Protein: 23.4
Fat: 5.5
Fiber: 10.4

Creamy (Or Chunky) Potato Chowder

Serves: 4 (or 1 person for 4 days)

Time: Around 30 minutes

Chowders are for cold nights, and this potato chowder (with a piece of crusty bread to mop up what I can't get with a spoon) is for the coldest of nights. Since it takes a bit longer than some of the other recipes in this section, I like to make it when I don't have much else to do, and can curl up with a bowl and watch my favorite TV show. It's truly comfort food.

Tip: *To make this a vegetarian soup, leave out bacon and replace condensed cream of chicken soup with condensed cream of mushroom.*

Ingredients:

Water (for boiling potatoes)

5 medium-sized Yukon Gold potatoes

½ pound bacon

¼ cup chopped red onion

One 12-oz can of corn kernels

One 10 ¾-oz can condensed cream of chicken soup

Salt to taste

Black pepper to taste

Directions:

Peel and chop the Yukon Gold potatoes. Add to a big stockpot and cover with water. Heat on high until you get a boil, then reduce to medium. Cook for 10-15 minutes until potatoes are easily pierced with a fork. Drain, but keep 1 cup of water.

While the potatoes are boiling, take care of the bacon and onion. In a skillet, cook the bacon until you get the crispiness you prefer. Remove bacon and set on a plate with paper towels. You want to keep the bacon grease in the pan. Chop onions and add to the greasy pan, cooking over medium-high until tenderized. Chop cooked bacon.

Add cooked potatoes, corn, onion, and cream of chicken soup to the stockpot with potato water. Turn heat to medium, until soup is warm. If you want a smooth, creamy soup, puree the whole thing and top with bacon. If you want a chunky soup, leave as is, and just stir in chopped bacon. Season.

In slow cooker:

Cook bacon and prep potatoes. Put potatoes, bacon, corn, and red onion in your slow cooker. Pour in just enough water (or substitute stock, which will make this a 6-ingredient soup) to cover the food. Cook on high for 7-8 hours or low for 3-4 hours.

Potatoes should be nice and tender. Add condensed cream of chicken soup and stir to heat through. Puree or leave chunky. Season and serve.

In pressure cooker:

Cook bacon and prep potatoes. Put potatoes, bacon, corn, and red onion into the pressure cooker. Pour in just enough water (or substitute stock) to cover the food, making sure it doesn't go over the maximum line in the pot. Seal the lid. Cook for 5 minutes. When time is up, wait 10 minutes or so, and then release any remaining pressure. Stir in cream of chicken soup and season to taste. Puree or leave chunky.

Nutritional Info (¼ recipe per serving):

Total calories: 582

Carbs: 54.9

Protein: 28.7

Fat: 28.9

Fiber: 4.1

Creamy Pea Soup

Serves: 3 (or 1 person for 3 days)

Time: About 20 minutes

A vibrant green that promises fresh flavors, this creamy pea soup is very easy to make and uses affordable ingredients like frozen peas. The first step doesn't actually involve the peas, however, it involves boiling a potato in chicken stock. The starchiness helps give the soup structure and richness. Then, you add the peas, and simmer. This is a pureed soup, so you will need a blender of some kind. Once smooth, swirl in Greek yogurt for creaminess, and top with peppery chopped radishes. Season with salt!

Ingredients:

1 baking potato

4 cups unsalted chicken stock

½ pound frozen peas

2 tablespoons plain Greek yogurt

1 chopped radish

Salt to taste

Directions:

Peel your baking potato and chop into reasonably-even pieces. Pour chicken stock into a big stockpot and add potato pieces. Bring to a simmer and cook for 12-15 minutes, until the potato is soft. Since this soup will be blended, it's okay if the potatoes get mushy. You definitely don't want them too firm.

Once potatoes are soft, add frozen peas and simmer for another 5 minutes or so, until they are heated through.

Blend soup until smooth. If the soup is too thick, add ¼ cup of chicken stock at a time, until you get the consistency you want. Season with salt to taste. Swirl a few spoonfuls of plain Greek yogurt into your soup and garnish with chopped radishes. Serve!

Nutritional Info (⅓ recipe per serving):

Total calories: 172

Carbs: 24.5

Protein: 16.5

Fat: 1.1

Fiber: 5.4

Creamy Broccoli-Cheddar Soup (Vegetarian)

Serves: 4 (or 1 person for 4 days)

Time: Around 15 minutes

A famous soup at a certain sandwich and bakery chain, broccoli + cheddar is really easy to make on your own. To get a really creamy texture, use evaporated milk. For seasonings, why nutmeg? It has a slightly sweet, nutty, and almost spicy flavor that pairs really well with the fattiness of evaporated milk and cheese.

Ingredients:

3 cups chicken stock

2 cups frozen broccoli florets

One 15-ounce can of evaporated milk

2 cups cheddar cheese

Pinch of nutmeg

Salt to taste

Directions:

In a stockpot, add chicken stock and broccoli florets. Heat on medium until it begins to boil. Reduce heat, just so it doesn't start a rolling boil, and cook for 5 minutes. When broccoli is tender, stir in evaporated milk and cook for another 2-3 minutes. Remove pot from heat and puree until smooth. Add cheese to melt, then season. Store leftovers no longer than 3-4 days.

Nutritional Info (¼ recipe per serving):

Total calories: 400

Carbs: 14.5

Protein: 22.6

Fat: 26.6

Fiber: 1

Under-The-Weather Chicken Noodle Soup

Serves: 3 (or 1 person for 3 days)
Time: 30-35 minutes

Whenever I'm feeling sick or recovering from illness, I want chicken noodle soup. It might be a universal health food. In this recipe, you're poaching the chicken instead of roasting it or cooking it in a skillet, so it gets really tender. Once cooked and shredded, simmer everything together in a pot for 15 minutes, and serve!

Ingredients:
Water (for poaching chicken)
2 chicken breasts
5 cups chicken stock
½ package of frozen mixed veggies
6-ounces of dry egg noodles
Italian seasoning to taste
Salt to taste

Directions:
Fill a pot with at least 1 ½-inches of water and season well with salt. Add chicken breasts and heat on medium-high until the water is simmering. Reduce the heat to low, then cover with a lid. Leave it alone for 15 minutes. Check the chicken with a thermometer - it should be at least 165-degrees. When the chicken has reached that temp, shred.

In a separate pot, pour in chicken stock, veggies, shredded chicken, noodles, Italian seasoning, and salt. Bring to a boil, then reduce heat to a simmer for 15 minutes or so, until noodles are tender. Serve!

In slow cooker:
Lay whole raw chicken breasts in the bottom of your slow cooker. Add the rest of the ingredients. Cook on low for 6-8 hours, or high for 4-5 hours. When time is up, shred the chicken with two forks. Taste and season with more salt if necessary.

In pressure cooker:
Pour chicken broth into the pressure cooker. Add chicken and seal the lid. Cook on high for 7 minutes. If you're using frozen breasts and haven't had a chance to defrost them, just increase to 12 minutes. When time is up, wait 5 minutes, then quick-release, and check the chicken. It should be easily shredded, and of course, at least 165-degrees. Hit the "sauté" button and add frozen veggies and noodles. Cook another 5 minutes or so, with the lid off, until noodles are soft and veggies are tender. Season and serve.

Nutritional Info (⅓ recipe per serving):
Total calories: 486
Carbs: 65
Protein: 33
Fat: 9.3
Fiber: 3.8

5-Ingredient Turkey Chili

Serves: 4 (or 1 person for 3 days)
Time: Around 30-35 minutes
A lot of chili recipes call for long, slow cooking, but most of us don't usually have the time for that. You can prepare a pot of turkey chili with tomatoes, beans, and chili powder in less than an hour, and while it probably won't taste quite like a chili that's been simmering for hours, it will definitely be tasty and satisfying.
Tip: *Because you're limited on ingredients and don't have a bunch of different spices around, the kind of chili powder you use matters. If you want a sweeter taste, go with a chili powder that contains cinnamon, sugar, and a mild pepper like red cayenne or Serrano. According to Epicurious, Spice Islands and Simply Organic both make powders with a bit of sweetness. If you like smoky flavors, look for powders with smoked paprika or chipotle.*

Ingredients:

1 tablespoon olive oil
1 pound ground turkey
Three 15-ounce cans of diced tomatoes
One 15-ounce can of drained beans
2 tablespoons chili powder (from a brand like Spice Islands)
Salt to taste

Directions:

Pour oil into a skillet and heat until shiny. Add turkey and cook until browned. Drain. In a stockpot, add tomatoes, beans, and cooked turkey. Heat on medium-high until boiling, then season well and reduce the heat. Cover pot with a lid and simmer for 10 minutes. When time is up, taste and season more if necessary. Leftovers should keep for three days.

In slow cooker:

Cook turkey as normal. Add to slow cooker with all the ingredients. Cook on low for 4-8 hours, depending on your schedule. Because the meat is already cooked, the slow cooker is basically just deepening the flavors.

In pressure cooker:

Cook turkey in olive oil in your pressure cooker, uncovered, on the "Sauté" setting. Add the rest of the ingredients and seal the lid. Adjust time to 15 minutes. When time is up, wait for the pressure to release naturally, about 10 minutes. If there's any pressure left, turn the valve. Taste and season more if necessary.

Nutritional Info (¼ recipe per serving):

Total calories: 342
Carbs: 20
Protein: 35.8
Fat: 16.7
Fiber: 7.4

CHAPTER 11: VEGAN

You've seen some vegan recipes and vegan variations scattered throughout the book so far, but here's a chapter dedicated to the diet. The requirement for a good vegan dish is flavor and nutrients. Because a vegan diet is so restrictive, you do have to be more intentional about getting good stuff like protein and iron. That's what I've tried to keep in mind when choosing recipes. I think flavor is just as important, though, since if it doesn't taste good, who will keep eating it? You'll find recipes for breakfasts, lunches, dinners, snacks, and desserts in this section.

Overnight Chia Breakfast Pudding

Serves: 1

Time: Overnight

Chia seeds are a great source of nutrients for vegans thanks to their fiber and protein count. When left in liquids, they transform from hard little seeds into larger, gel-like bulbs, giving whatever liquid they were in a pudding texture. In this recipe, that liquid is almond milk, but it can be whatever non-dairy milk you prefer. It soaks overnight, and then you add maple syrup for sweetener and whatever fruit you have around. You can also use granola if you want a texture contrast.

Ingredients:

½ cup unsweetened almond milk

1 tablespoon of chia seeds

1 teaspoon maple syrup

Small handful of fresh fruit

Directions:

Mix milk and chia seeds in a big mug or Mason jar. Stick in the fridge overnight. When you're ready for breakfast, take out the pudding. You'll see the seeds have absorbed a lot of the milk and are now squishy. Stir in maple syrup and serve with fruit.

Nutritional Info (1 pudding):

Total calories: 139

Carbs: 19.8

Protein: 4.2

Fat: 6.7

Fiber: 10.5

Breakfast Burrito

Serves: 1

Time: Less than 5 minutes

When I'm really hungry in the morning, I like breakfast burritos. In this vegan version, the filling is made of cooked white rice and beans (which make a complete protein) mixed with salsa and wrapped up with avocado. You can use whatever salsa you want, depending on how spicy you like your burritos. The filling gets warmed up in the microwave for really fast cooking, so this is a great breakfast if you don't have a ton of time.

Tip: *You will need rice that's already cooked for this recipe. As a vegan, you should always have cooked rice on hand for fast meals.*

Ingredients:

½ cup cooked white rice

½ cup canned and drained black beans

½ cup salsa

1 small avocado

1 flour tortilla

Salt to taste

Black pepper to taste

Directions:

In a bowl, mix white rice, black beans, and salsa. Stick in the microwave to heat up, about 40 seconds or so. When ready, taste and season as needed.

Slice the avocado. Lay out your tortilla and spoon in the rice/bean/salsa mixture. Add avocado slices and wrap the burrito. Enjoy!

Nutritional Info (1 burrito):

Total calories: 552

Carbs: 70

Protein: 12.5

Fat: 28.2

Fiber: 18.9

Black Bean Burgers

Serves: 2

Time: 15-20 minutes

You can find lots of meat-free burgers at the store, but they aren't always cheap, and they're usually pretty processed. Making your own is very easy - you just need beans, breadcrumbs, zucchini, and some spices. Mushing most of the beans gives you a paste that helps hold the burger together; it's like mortar holding bricks (the whole beans). Breadcrumbs also help with the structure, while zucchini adds moisture. Fry your patties in a skillet and serve like a normal burger!

Ingredients:

1 ⅓ cups drained black beans

2 tablespoons dry breadcrumbs (Panko is great)

½ zucchini

½ tablespoon taco seasoning

Salt to taste

Cooking spray

Directions:

With a fork, mush all but a small handful of the black beans and mix with breadcrumbs. Add the whole black beans and set aside for now.

With a cheese grater, grate zucchini. Wrap in a paper towel and really squeeze out the liquid. You want the zucchini as dry as possible.

Add grated zucchini to the black bean mixture. Season with taco seasoning and salt. With clean hands, form burger patties. Spray a skillet with cooking spray and heat. When hot, add burgers and cook for 6 minutes on one side. Flip, and cook another 4 minutes or so.

Serve on buns with toppings or on a green salad.

Nutritional Info (½ recipe per serving):

Total calories: 108

Carbs: 19.2

Protein: 7.2

Fat: 0.5

Fiber: 6.6

Tofu Pasta with Broccoli

Serves: 2

Time: Around 15 minutes

For a quick pasta dinner, this is a great go-to recipe for vegans. You're basically replacing the usual chicken with tofu, which cooks much quicker in a skillet with olive oil and plenty of salt and pepper. I like broccoli in pasta, but you can use any frozen vegetable.

Tip: *You can leave out broccoli if you want, and pour in some marinara sauce for a take on classic spaghetti.*

Ingredients:

8-ounces extra firm tofu

½ pound dry spaghetti pasta

¼ cup olive oil

2 cups of frozen broccoli

Dried garlic to taste

Water (for boiling)

Salt to taste

Black pepper to taste

Directions:

Drain tofu and dry with paper towels. You'll have to push down a little on the block to get the water out. Cut into cubes.

Boil water and prepare pasta according to directions on the box. It should take about 6-7 minutes.

In a skillet, heat olive oil until shiny. Add tofu and cook, stirring, until it's turning golden and getting crispy. Sprinkle in a little salt and stir. Set aside for now.

Put broccoli in a colander in the sink, and pour the hot pasta water over it, keeping the pasta in the pot with another colander. Move broccoli to pasta and stir, until heated through. Add tofu and toss everything with dried garlic, salt, and pepper to taste.

Nutritional Info (½ recipe per serving):

Total calories: 842

Carbs: 93

Protein: 31

Fat: 40

Fiber: 6.4

Baked Buffalo Cauliflower

Serves: 2-3

Time: Less than 30 minutes

Buffalo wings have a distinct silky-hot flavor thanks to hot sauce and butter. While normally a sauce for chicken, cauliflower is a really tasty and vegan alternative. Cauliflower only needs about 20 minutes to cook in a very hot oven, and then you toss with homemade buffalo sauce prepared with a vegan butter substitute. Season and enjoy!

Ingredients:

1 head of cauliflower

3 tablespoons melted vegan butter (divided)

1/2 cup hot sauce

Salt to taste

Black pepper to taste

Directions:

Preheat your oven to 450-degrees. Break up the cauliflower into florets with clean hands and toss with 1 tablespoon of melted butter substitute, salt, and pepper. When the oven is hot, spread the cauliflower on a baking sheet and roast for 20 minutes, until easily-pierced with a fork.

In a bowl, whisk ½ cup of hot sauce with the rest of the melted vegan butter. Pour over the cauliflower and toss, so the florets are well-coated. When cool enough, taste, and add more salt and pepper if needed.

Nutritional Info (½ recipe):

Total calories: 189

Carbs: 8

Protein: 2.9

Fat: 16.9

Fiber: 3.5

Simple Lentil Chili (Vegan)

Serves: 4 (or 1 person for 4 days)

Time: 15-20 minutes

A lot of chilis are really meaty, but if you're vegan, meat is out. Instead, use lentils, which are legumes packed with nutrients like protein and fiber. We're going with lentils in a can (unless you're cooking in a slow cooker or pressure cooker), so you don't have to bother cooking dry ones. Simmer with tomatoes, vegetable broth, onion, salt, and plenty of chili powder.

Ingredients:

Two 14-ounce cans of chopped tomatoes

4 cups vegetable broth

½ chopped onion

1 cup canned lentils

Chili powder to taste

Salt to taste

Directions:

Pour tomatoes and broth into the stockpot. Add onions, lentils, and chili powder. Heat on medium-high until boiling, then reduce. Simmer with the lid on for 15 minutes. Season to taste with salt. Leftovers will keep for around 4 days.

In slow cooker:

Replace canned lentils with dry lentils if you're making it in the slow cooker. Put everything in the slow cooker and cook on high for 3-4 hours, or low for 7-8 hours. Taste and season with more salt if necessary.

In pressure cooker:

Replace canned lentils with dry lentils. Pour everything into the pressure cooker. Adjust time to 15 minutes. When time is up, wait for a natural pressure release. Taste and season with more salt if necessary.

Nutritional Info (¼ recipe per serving):

Total calories: 550

Carbs: 119.5

Protein: 22.8

Fat: 3.6

Fiber: 32.7

Taco-Seasoned Roasted Chickpeas

Makes: 3 cups

Time: 40-60 minutes

Chickpeas are bite-sized and when baked for long enough, they become crunchy. They're basically chips! Roasted chickpeas have definitely become popular in recent years, and there are endless flavor combinations, like cinnamon sugar. For this recipe, we're staying savory, and using just olive oil and a good taco seasoning. You know chickpeas are roasted thoroughly when they are crunchy all the way through.

Ingredients:

Two 15-ounce cans of cooked chickpeas

1 ½ tablespoons olive oil

2 teaspoons taco seasoning

Salt to taste

Black pepper to taste

Directions:

Preheat oven to 375-degrees and line a cookie sheet with parchment paper. Drain and rinse your chickpeas, and then dry really well. You want them as dry as possible. Put chickpeas on baking sheet and bake for 10-15 minutes. Move to a bowl, and carefully toss with olive oil, salt, pepper, and taco seasoning. They will be hot. Return to the baking sheet and roast another 20-25 minutes, until brown. When the timer goes off, keep them in the oven for another 10-20 minutes. This will help them dry out even more, because you want them crunchy.

Serve and enjoy! If there's leftovers, store in an airtight container for no longer than 2 days.

Nutritional Info (½ cup recipe per serving):

Total calories: 199

Carbs: 32.1

Protein: 7

Fat: 5.1

Fiber: 6.2

Rice 'n Bean Enchiladas

Serves: 2

Time: 25 minutes

Enchiladas are a great vegan dish because they are very versatile and really quick. In this recipe, we're using the classic combo of rice and beans, which together make a complete protein. This is a great way to use up cooked white rice, though if you don't have any on hand, you can substitute with tofu or veggies.

Ingredients:

2 whole-wheat tortillas (vegan)

1 cup cooked rice

1 cup drained beans

1 cup of vegan shredded cheese

1 cup enchilada sauce

Salt to taste

Black pepper to taste

Directions:

Preheat your oven to 350-degrees. In a bowl, mix cooked rice and beans with salt and pepper to taste. Spread out your tortillas on a sprayed baking sheet and fill with rice and bean mixture, cheese, and around ¼ cup of the enchilada sauce per tortilla. Roll up and pour over the rest of the sauce. Bake for 20 minutes or so. Enjoy!

Nutritional Info (½ recipe per serving):

Total calories: 436

Carbs: 69.6

Protein: 9.8

Fat: 13.1

Fiber: 5.7

Cookie Dough Bites

Makes: 6 bites

Time: Less than 10 minutes

I like eating cookie dough right out of the bowl, but I don't always want to make cookies for that. Eating raw cookie dough is also not super safe. For a safe and easy alternative, there are these cookie dough bites! You'll need one ripe banana, peanut butter, vanilla, oats, chocolate chips, and then just a pinch of salt to bring all the flavors together. This recipe makes six little bites, so if you want more to share, just double the recipe.

Ingredients:

1 ripe banana

2 ½ tablespoons creamy-style (or chunky) peanut butter

Splash of vanilla

1 ¼ cups oats

3 tablespoons mini dairy-free chocolate chips

Pinch of salt

Directions:

In a bowl, mash your banana with a wooden spoon. Add peanut butter and vanilla. Mix until combined. Stir in oats, chocolate chips, and salt. With clean hands, form into 6 balls, and refrigerate. When firm, they're ready to eat! Eat these within the next 4-5 days, if they last that long!

Nutritional Info (1 bite per serving):

Total calories: 200

Carbs: 23.2

Protein: 6.3

Fat: 10.4

Fiber: 3.5

Lemon-Coconut Bites

Makes: 6 bites

Time: Less than 10 minutes

When you want something light and sweet, these are the perfect bites of sunshine. The "dough" is totally vegan: just dates and almonds. The dates should be soft, so if they're too hard, soak in warm water for a while. After blitzing the almonds and dates down into a dough, add shredded coconut and lemon juice. If you think you'll want more than six bites over the next few days, the recipe is easily doubled.

Tip: *You will need a food processor or blender for this recipe.*

Ingredients:

½ cup almonds

½ cup softened dates

5 tablespoons shredded coconut

1 tablespoon lemon juice

Directions:

Put almonds in your food processor and pulse until the pieces are really small. It doesn't have to be powder, but more flour-like than not. Add dates and pulse again until you get a dough texture.

Add coconut and lemon juice. Pulse again. With clean hands, mold into 6 balls. Store in the fridge to harden up a little before enjoying. To make them last longer, keep in the freezer. Eat within 4-5 days.

Nutritional Info (1 bite per serving):

Total calories: 103

Carbs: 13.5

Protein: 2.2

Fat: 5.4

Fiber: 2.6

CHAPTER 12: SNACKS

When I was in college, I participated in intramural sports, so I was frequently hungry. My first year, I noticed I was spending a lot of money on snacks from vending machines or the store, so I started brainstorming nibbles I could make myself. This section is full of healthy, homemade sweet and savory snacks, many of which require zero cooking. College student or not, if you always find yourself hunting around for food, or want to break out from the potato chip/candy/junk food routine, you'll love these recipes.

Pita Bread Pizza

Serves: 1-2

Time: Less than 10 minutes

For a snack that's basically a miniature meal, pita bread pizzas are pretty great. Like all pizzas, you can customize toppings to your liking, so you don't need to use pepperoni and olives. You can just stick with cheese and add cheddar to the mozzarella if you want, or throw some leftover roasted veggies on there, if you have them. Pizza will serve 1-2 people, depending on how hungry you are.

Ingredients:

1 pita bread

2 tablespoons red sauce

Handful of mozzarella cheese

Handful of pepperoni slices

Handful of black olives

Directions:

Preheat oven to 400-degrees. Assemble pizza by spooning sauce on the pita, followed by cheese, pepperoni, and olives. Bake for just 5-7 minutes, until the cheese is melty. Enjoy!

Nutritional Info (1 recipe):

Total calories: 378

Carbs: 37.6

Protein: 16.4

Fat: 17.6

Fiber: 2.3

Stuffed Dates (Vegetarian)

Serves: 1-2

Time: Less than 5 minutes

Dates are a really great snack food and full of nutrients like fiber and antioxidants. They're also naturally quite sweet and almost jam-like in their flavor, which makes them the perfect vehicle for peanut butter! Sprinkle on a little salt (if your peanut butter isn't salted) and enjoy!

Ingredients:

4 Medjool dates

2 tablespoons peanut butter

Sprinkle of salt

Directions:

Split the dates and remove the pit. With a spoon, stuff dates with peanut butter. Top with a sprinkle of salt.

Nutritional Info (½ recipe):

Total calories: 254

Carbs: 45.2

Protein: 6

Fat: 8.1

Fiber: 5

Cottage Cheese Parfait (Vegetarian)

Serves: 1

Time: Less than 5 minutes

Cottage cheese is great because it can be either sweet or savory, depending on what you put in it. I like combining the two with sliced avocado and honey, which is also a favorite toast combo of mine. A sprinkle of salt brings the flavors together.

Tip: *If you think avocado with cottage cheese is weird, you can use berries instead. Blueberries are my favorite.*

Ingredients:

½ avocado

1 cup cottage cheese

Drizzle of honey

Pinch of salt

Directions:

Carefully cut the avocado in half and remove the pit. Wrap one half in tinfoil and store in the fridge for later. With a spoon, remove the avocado from its shell and slice.

Spoon cottage cheese into a dish or glass and top with avocado. Drizzle with honey and a sprinkle of salt. Stir, then enjoy!

Nutritional Info (1 parfait):

Total calories: 369

Carbs: 21.4

Protein: 32.8

Fat: 17.7

Fiber: 5.9

Greek Yogurt Dip (Vegetarian)

Serves: 1

Time: Less than 5 minutes

This dip, which is awesome with veggies or slices of pita, borrows flavors from tzatziki, the traditional Greek yogurt sauce that comes on gyros. Freshness comes from grated cucumber and Italian seasoning, while lemon juice adds acid to cut through the richness of the yogurt. For the best flavor, eat up the dip within a day of making it.

Ingredients:

¼ cucumber

1 cup Greek yogurt

Italian seasoning to taste

Squeeze of lemon juice

Sliced raw vegetables (to serve)

Directions:

Grate your cucumber (you can just use a cheese grater) into the yogurt. Add Italian seasoning to taste, and then squeeze in lemon juice, or use ½ tablespoon or so of bottled lemon juice. Serve with sliced vegetables, like celery, bell peppers, and carrots and/or slices of warmed pita bread.

Nutritional Info (1 recipe of dip per serving):

Total calories: 141

Carbs: 13.7

Protein: 22.5

Fat: 0.1

Fiber: 0.4

Peanut Butter Energy Balls (Vegetarian)

Makes: 20 balls

Time: 20-25 minutes

You can find a bazillion recipes for energy balls on the internet, but they all generally share five basic Ingredients oats, dried fruit, nut butter, sweetener, and mix-ins. In this recipe, I've chosen peanut butter as the nut butter and honey for the sweetener because both are must-haves for college students. For fruit, I really like dried apricots, but dates are very popular, too. For mix-ins, crushed nuts is a classic, but you can also use chia seeds, dried coconut, ground flax, mini chocolate chips, and so on. Let your imagination run wild.

Ingredients:

1 cup rolled oats

½ cup dried apricots (or dates)

½ cup peanut butter

¼ cup honey

¼ cup crushed nuts

Tip: *To make this vegan, use agave instead of honey.*

Directions:

Put oats in a food processor and grind until fine, like flour. Add the rest of the ingredients and pulse until you get a sticky "dough."

Using clean hands, roll 1 tablespoon of dough at a time into balls. Line a baking sheet with parchment paper and lay energy balls on it. Freeze until solid, or about 15-20 minutes. Put balls in a freezer bag to store. They'll last up to 3 months! If you want some, just let them sit at room temperature a little while, so they soften nicely.

Nutritional Info (2 balls per serving):

Total calories: 171

Carbs: 22.3

Protein: 5.1

Fat: 8.2

Fiber: 2.6

Basic Honey Granola (Vegetarian)

Makes: 3 cups

Time: 30-35 minutes

Granola is one of my favorite snacks and it's so versatile. It can be eaten as cereal with a bowl of milk, layered with yogurt for a parfait, or just eaten out of a bag while walking across campus. It's surprisingly-easy to make yourself, too. Just plan on using the oven for at least 30 minutes.

Ingredients:

3 cups rolled oats

⅓ cup honey

½ teaspoon ground cinnamon

Mix-ins (raisins, chocolate chips, or dried fruit)

Salt to taste

Tip: *To make this granola vegan, replace honey with agave.*

Directions:

Preheat oven to 300 degrees and line a cookie sheet with parchment paper.

In a bowl, mix oats with honey and cinnamon. I like to coat my hands with some cooking spray, and then toss the oats. Thanks to the spray, there isn't too much stickage. When the oats are thoroughly coated, spread on your baking sheet in an even layer.

Bake for 15 minutes, then stir the oats around, so they don't burn. Bake for another 15 minutes or so. The oats will smell toasty and will be starting to brown. They continue to bake a little out of the oven, because of the residual heat. The granola will also get much crunchier as it cools. Stir in your salt and mix-in. Start with less salt than you think you need, and then taste. I've made too-salty granola before, and it is not very pleasant. Once you've gotten the flavor you want, store granola in an airtight container. It should keep for about 2-3 weeks.

Nutritional Info (½ cup plain granola per serving):

Total calories: 212

Carbs: 43.2

Protein: 5.4

Fat: 2.7

Fiber: 4.2

Stovetop Buttery Popcorn

Serves: 1-2

Time: Less than 10 minutes

Stovetop popcorn really doesn't take much longer than the microwave kind, and I've found that it's always better for some reason. Maybe that's just because I feel more accomplished, but I think the fact that I'm adding my own butter and salt makes a difference, too. All you need to make popcorn from kernels is hot oil, a pot, and a lid. The key is to test the hot oil with just a few kernels first, and then when they pop, add the rest in and remove the pot from the heat. This lets the kernels all get to relatively the same temperature, so when you put the pot back on the stove, they all pop at once. This way, none of them will burn.

Ingredients:

3 tablespoons olive oil

3 tablespoons popcorn kernels (makes about 6 cups)

1 tablespoon melted butter

Salt to taste

Directions:

Pour oil into a pot (at least 3 quarts for the amount of popcorn we're making) and heat on medium. When shiny, add 2-3 kernels and wait for them to pop. When they do, add the rest of the kernels, making sure they're in an even layer. Put the lid on the pot and hold it away from the heat. Wait about 30 seconds.

After 30 seconds, return pot to the heat. Kernels should begin popping all at once. You can shake the pan (carefully) to make sure all the kernels are contacting the hot pot bottom. Once the popping starts to die down, dump the popcorn in a bowl.

Toss with melted butter and salt to taste.

Everything Bagel variation:

Instead of salt, toss buttered popcorn with Everything Seasoning from a brand like Trader Joe's.

Taco variation:

After drizzling on butter, toss popcorn with taco seasoning.

Garlic-herb:

After drizzling on butter, toss popcorn with salt, garlic powder, and Italian seasoning.

Nutritional info (1 recipe):

Total calories: 351

Carbs: 29

Protein: 4

Fat: 28

Fiber: 6

Banana Chips (Vegan)

Serves: 2

Time: 3-4 hours

Of the dried fruits, banana is underrated. The natural sugars are so strong and the flavor gets more concentrated. I love to eat banana chips on their own or added to granola. They can even be broken up and used in cookies or brownies. Because banana chips need to be dried at a low temperature, it does take a few hours. Make these on a day when you know no one else needs the oven for a while.

Ingredients:

5 big ripe bananas

4 tablespoons lemon juice

Sprinkle of cinnamon

Directions:

Preheat the oven to 200-degrees. Line a cookie sheet with parchment paper. While the oven preheats, peel bananas and slice into coins about ¼-inch thick. Dip in lemon juice and place on the cookie sheet. Sprinkle all the coins with cinnamon. Bake for 1 ½ hours, then flip coins over. After 3-4 hours total, the chips should be dry and a little brown. Cool before eating or storing in an airtight container. They should last about a week.

Nutritional Info (½ recipe per serving):

Total calories: 268

Carbs: 67.9

Protein: 3.4

Fat: 1.2

Fiber: 7.8

CHAPTER 13: DRINKS

Staying hydrated is very important no matter what stage of life you're in, but it can be something a college student forgets when juggling a hectic struggle. Obviously, water is the best drink of choice at any given time, but it gets boring. Rather than spending your money on unhealthy soft drinks or expensive juices, why not make your own? These drinks are also great for serving at parties.

Classic Iced Tea

Serves: 2-3

Time: Less than 15 minutes (cold brew method is overnight)

When water is boring, iced tea can come to the rescue. This recipe works for any tea, whether it's black, green, oolong, or white. Black tea is a good replacement for coffee since it has caffeine, while green tea is great for those trying a healthier lifestyle. For a classic black iced tea, sugar is the usual sweetener, while green tea and honey are awesome. It's really up to you, though, and your personal tastes. If you want to cold-brew your tea, there are instructions for that method at the end of the recipe.

Ingredients:

4 bags of your favorite tea

1-2 ½ tablespoons of honey (or sugar)

1 lemon

2 cups hot water

2 cups ice cubes

1 cup cold water

Directions:

Get the water heating up, and when at the right temperature, add the four tea bags. You can be really exact with the temperature if you want, using a thermometer, or you can just guess based on what should be brewed hotter or cooler. Brew according to the time on the instructions below.

Black tea - 3-5 minutes/190-210 °F

Herbal tea - 3-5 minutes/190-210 °F

Green tea - 1-3 minutes/170-180 °F

White tea - 3-4 minutes/170-180 °F

Oolong tea - 3-5 minutes/170-180 °F

When brewing time is up, take out the bags carefully, then whisk in honey or sugar to blend. Cool tea to room temperature. Divide ice into the glasses or jars you're serving in, or put in a pitcher. Pour in the lukewarm tea, and then pour in the cold water. Slice the lemon in half and give the tea a good squirt. If the tea is not cold enough to your liking, refrigerate a bit longer before enjoying.

Cold brew method:

A lot of people like to cold-brew their tea. Why? It can result in more natural sweetness, since hot water can accentuate tea's bitterness. It's a pretty easy process. Just put your four tea bags in 3 cups of cold water with the ice, and keep in the fridge for about 8 hours or overnight. To sweeten, first mix honey or sugar in a little warm water until it dissolves, then add to the cold brew. Serve with lemon.

Nutritional Info (1 cup):

Total calories: 52

Carbs: 13.3

Protein: 0.2

Fat: 0

Fiber: 0

Classic Lemonade

Serves: 6

Time: 10-40 minutes (if chilling)

Real lemonade is just three Ingredients water, sugar, and lemon juice. For a really evenly-sweetened lemonade, a simple syrup is the way to go. You just heat water and sugar together, and then mix with cold water and lemon juice. This base lemonade can be customized in an endless variety of ways. I've given instructions on strawberry and raspberry lemonade - two classics - but you could use mixed berries, blueberries, peaches, cherries, and more.

Ingredients:

6 cups water

⅓ cup sugar

1 cup fresh lemon juice

Directions:

Pour 1 cup of water into a saucepan and add sugar. Heat on medium-high, stirring, until the sugar dissolves. Set your simple syrup aside for now to cool a bit.

Get out a pitcher and add lemon juice. Pour in simple syrup and then 5 cups of very cold water. Stir well. If you want a really chill drink, stick in the fridge for a half hour or so. Serve over ice!

Strawberry-lemonade variation:

Make the lemonade as normal. Now, get 1 pound or so of strawberries (fresh or frozen) and put in a saucepan. Heat on low or medium, and mash strawberries with the back of a wooden spoon or spatula, so they start to release their juices. If they're frozen, they'll take a little longer to get soft. Once softened and juicy, transfer to your lemonade pitcher, stir, and chill.

Raspberry-lemonade variation:

Make the lemonade as normal. Get 2 cups of raspberries (fresh or frozen) and heat in a saucepan over low/medium. As they soften, mush with a wooden spoon or spatula. Pour into your prepared lemonade, stir, and chill.

Nutritional Info (1 cup):

Total calories: 51

Carbs: 12

Protein: 0

Fat: 0

Fiber: 0

Basil-Peach Arnold Palmer

Serves: 1-2 (syrup makes enough for 8)

Time: About 46 minutes (to prepare syrup from scratch)

While this recipe seems long for a drink, it's worth it. The ingredient measurements for the syrup make 1 cup, or about eight servings. It keeps in the fridge for up to a month, which is days and days of refreshing lemonades, teas, and Arnold Palmers. If you aren't sure if you'll love the syrup, it's easy to reduce the ingredients. I love basil and peach together, and I love Arnold Palmers, so this drink calls my name on hot days. If the syrup is already made, this recipe will take at max (if you're brewing a fresh unsweetened tea) 10 minutes or so. If you already have both the tea and syrup done, it's like one minute.

Tip: *To make this Arnold Palmer, you'll need iced tea before it's been sweetened. You can either keep one cup or two unsweetened when you make a big batch, or brew tea specifically for this recipe. Brewing a bag of tea won't add too much time to the recipe; you can easily do it while the syrup is cooling.*

Ingredients:

1 cup white sugar

1 cup fresh basil leaves

1 cup water

½ ripe peach

¾ cup brewed iced tea (unsweetened)

¾ cup of classic lemonade

Directions:

In a small saucepan, mix sugar, fresh basil, and water. On medium, bring to a boil, stirring the whole time, to dissolve the sugar. Reduce to low and simmer for just a minute or so. Steep the syrup for 30 minutes.

While that's steeping, put ½ peach in another saucepan and heat on low. Feel free to eat the other half while you're finishing up the Arnold Palmer recipe. Mush up the slices in the saucepan a little, so they start to break down and release their juices. Pour into a large glass and fill with ¾ cup unsweetened iced tea and ¾ cup lemonade. If you're making two Arnold Palmers, just eyeball the division. Store in the fridge to chill for now.

When syrup is cool, pour through a fine mesh strainer into a clean jar. Sweeten your peach Arnold Palmer(s) with 1-2 tablespoons of syrup per glass. Start with just one tablespoon and taste. Seal the syrup jar and store in the fridge for up to one month.

Nutritional Info (1 ½ cups basil syrup-sweetened peach Arnold Palmer):

Total calories: 64

Carbs: 15.1

Protein: 0.5

Fat: 0

Fiber: 0

Sweet Iced Coffee

Serves: 1

Time: About 15 minutes

In college, I knew some people who couldn't really get going until they had their coffee. One girl from an English class always had an iced coffee, no matter what temperature it was outside. If you're like her, but don't want to spend the money at a cafe, here's a recipe for your own. You will need a coffee machine, or you could buy a hot black coffee somewhere. That will be pretty cheap, and then you can transform it into iced coffee.

Ingredients:

1 cup brewed coffee

2 tablespoons sugar

2 tablespoons water

Handful of ice

Heavy cream to taste

Directions:

Brew coffee as you would normally, then set aside in a mug to cool. Put it in the fridge if you want it to cool faster. While the coffee cools, start the simple syrup. Mix sugar and water in a medium saucepan and heat on medium, stirring constantly, until the sugar dissolves. Let this cool.

By now, the coffee should be cool. Sweeten coffee with simple syrup. Put some ice in a glass and pour in the coffee. Add as much cream as you would like, if you don't want black iced coffee.

Nutritional Info (1 recipe per serving):

Total calories: 144

Carbs: 24.4

Protein: 0

Fat: 0

Fiber: 0

Orange Punch

Serves: 5

Time: About 5 minutes

This bright-colored, energizing orange punch is the perfect drink for parties and so easy to put together. All you need is sugar, a little lime juice, white grape juice, oranges, and club soda. If you find white grape juice sweet enough on its own, you can even skip the sugar.

Ingredients:

¼ cup sugar

¼ cup lime juice

4 cups cold white grape juice

Three large ripe oranges

½ liter cold club soda

Ice cubes

Directions:

Get a big pitcher or bowl for the punch. Whisk sugar and lime juice together until dissolved. Pour in grape juice.

Cut two of the oranges in half and squeeze out as much juice as you can into the punch. Slice the third and put the slices in the pitcher or bowl.

Pour in club soda, stir, and serve with ice cubes to keep the punch cold.

Nutritional Info (⅕ recipe):

Total calories: 169

Carbs: 42

Protein: 2.1

Fat: 0

Fiber: 0

Cranberry Punch

Serves: 8

Time: 5 minutes

This big-batch punch is perfect for gatherings like Thanksgiving or autumn-themed parties. Cranberries are in season, and it should be pretty easy to find frozen ones. If you can't, just use a sliced orange as your punch garnish. All the juices and ginger ale should be kept cold, so the punch is ready to serve right after you mix it. Because ginger ale and orange juice are sugary on their own, you shouldn't need to add any sweeteners.

Ingredients:

32-ounces cold cranberry juice

2 cups of cold orange juice

2 cups chilled ginger ale

1 sliced orange or a couple of handfuls of frozen cranberries

Ice cubes

Directions:

Get out a big pitcher or punch bowl. Mix cranberry juice and orange juice together. Pour in ginger ale and orange slices or frozen cranberries. Serve right away with ice cubes.

Nutritional Info (⅛ recipe):

Total calories: 125

Carbs: 25.8

Protein: 0

Fat: 0

Fiber: 0

Classic Hot Chocolate

Serves: 2

Time: Less than 10 minutes

On winter days, I'll find myself craving hot chocolate. While you could always use boxed or packet mixes, the cheap ones don't taste very good, and the good ones are too expensive. Why not just make it yourself? You probably have the ingredients already, and it takes less than 10 minutes on the stovetop to make enough for you and a friend.

Ingredients:

Dash of salt

¼ cup sugar

2 tablespoons baking cocoa

2 ½ tablespoons water

2 cups milk

Tip: *To make this non-dairy, sub out cow's milk for almond, coconut, or soy milk.*

Directions:

Mix dash of salt, sugar, and cocoa in a saucepan. Add water and bring to a boil on medium heat. Let this boil for 2 minutes, then reduce the heat. Pour in milk, which will cool down the liquid, and stir. Heat to the temperature you like to drink your hot chocolate, making sure it doesn't boil, and then give it one more good stir before enjoying!

Nutritional Info (½ recipe):

Total calories: 228

Carbs: 39.9

Protein: 9.1

Fat: 5.7

Fiber: 1.8

2-Ingredient Nutella Hot Chocolate

Serves: 2

Time: Less than 10 minutes

Extremely-rich and easy, this hot chocolate uses just milk and Nutella. Heat together on the stovetop, whisking so it stays smooth, and drink when warmed to your liking. If you want, you can add whipped cream, but I think it's just perfect without any frills.

Ingredients:

1 ½ cups milk

5 tablespoons Nutella

Directions:

Add milk and Nutella to a saucepan. Heat on medium, whisking, until the hot chocolate is simmering. Serve! If you have whipped cream around, feel free to indulge.

Nutritional Info (½ recipe):

Total calories: 312

Carbs: 34.3

Protein: 8.2

Fat: 15.9

Fiber: 2.2

Chai Tea Latte

Serves: 1-2

Time: Less than 10 minutes

If I had to pick a favorite beverage, it would be chai tea lattes. The spiced, milky drink always makes me happy on cold days, and the iced version is my ideal pick-me-up during hot summer months. When I was in college, I couldn't find a decent chai latte within walking distance to save my life, so I ended up just figuring out how to make my own. It was surprisingly easy, and you only need four Ingredients tea bags, milk, water, and sugar.

Tip: *You can make your own chai spice mix from scratch (cinnamon, ginger, nutmeg, cardamom, cloves, allspice) and add to brewed black tea, but it's just more convenient to use chai tea bags. If you make chai constantly, and are always buying bags, it is cheaper to just buy the spices, so keep that in mind.*

Ingredients:

¼ cup water

2 chai tea bags

¾ cup warm milk

Sugar to taste

Directions:

Bring water to a boil. Add tea bags and steep for 3-5 minutes. While that heats up, warm the milk either in the microwave (starting with just 15 seconds) or in another saucepan on the stovetop.

When tea is ready, pour into mug(s) and pour in milk. Sweeten to taste, and serve!

Tip: *Chai not strong enough for you? You can simmer tea bags longer for a more concentrated flavor - just bring water to a simmer, add bags, and simmer on low for 10 minutes.*

Iced chai variation:

Bring water to a boil and steep tea as usual. Add sugar when tea is still hot, so it dissolves. Put sweetened tea in the fridge to chill. When cool, pour over ice and then pour in cold milk.

Nutritional Info (1 recipe w/ 2 tablespoons of sugar):

Total calories: 182

Carbs: 33

Protein: 6

Fat: 3.8

Fiber: 0

Mulled Cider

Serves: 8

Time: 35 minutes - 1 hour, 30 minutes (if using slow cooker)

Mulled cider is a classic Christmas drink that will make any college student feel grown up. This is a non-alcoholic version that just uses good ol' apple cider, which is a fancy word for unfiltered apple juice. I like it better for mulled cider, it's richer and less processed, but in a pinch, you could use regular apple juice. Instead of dealing with a handful of spices you probably wouldn't use for anything else (cinnamon sticks, cardamom pods, etc.), I'm recommending getting a mulling spice mix kit. Amazon sells them from brands like Spice Islands for about $5.

Tip: *Unless you're making mulled cider every weekend, you probably won't use up all the spice mix. Since spices last a long time and don't go bad, you could keep them around for next year, but they might not be as potent. To put them to use now, put remaining spice into little jars or Christmas baggies, and give away as gifts!*

Ingredients:

½ gallon apple cider

Mulling spice mix kit

1 orange

Directions:

Pour cider into a large stockpot on the stove. Add spices. How much depends on the kit you're using. As an example, the Spice Islands kit comes with an infuser ball, and has you fill it with 2 teaspoons of spices for every quart of cider. For this recipe, that would be 2 quarts, so 4 teaspoons. Feel free to add more if you like a really mulled, spiced flavor.

Slice an orange and toss in the cider. Bring spiced apple cider to a boil on medium-high heat, then reduce to simmer. Simmer for 30 minutes.

If you didn't have an infuser and there's spices floating around in the cider, strain. Serve cider warm, keeping in the orange slices as garnish.

In slow cooker:

Instead of a stockpot, put cider, spices, and orange in a slow cooker (or multi-cooker on the slow cooker setting). Heat on "high" for 30 minutes, then switch to "low" for an hour. Serve!

Nutritional Info (⅛ recipe per serving):

Total calories: 127

Carbs: 31.7

Protein: 0

Fat: 0

Fiber: 0

CHAPTER 14: DESSERTS

If you're like me, you are very excited to reach this section. I'm a big believer in the healing power of a good dessert, and I believe there's nothing wrong with a little real sugar, butter, and chocolate. I do understand the desire to be healthier, though, and use alternative ingredients, so many of these recipes embrace stuff like avocado, bananas, oats, and more.

Avocado Chocolate Mousse

Serves: 1-2

Time: 35 minutes

When I crave something chocolatey, I always think of chocolate mousse. It's light, creamy, and when it's really cold, it's great for hot evenings. Avocados are actually the perfect base thanks to their fattiness and neutral flavor. Simply mix a blended avocado with honey, cocoa powder, milk, and vanilla for an easy chocolate dessert that looks really impressive, and has vitamins and minerals!

Tip: *To make this dairy-free, use almond, coconut, or soy milk.*

Ingredients:

1 avocado

¼ cup honey

¼ cup unsweetened cocoa powder

4 tablespoons milk

1 teaspoon pure vanilla extract

Tip: *To substitute honey, use just 1 teaspoon of stevia liquid concentrate.*

Directions:

Carefully cut the avocado and remove the pit. Scoop out the flesh with a spoon and put in a food processor or smoothie blender. Add honey, cocoa, milk, and vanilla. Blend until smooth and creamy. Chill in the fridge for about a half hour, then serve!

Nutritional Info (1 recipe per serving):

Total calories: 626

Carbs: 99.5

Protein: 9.9

Fat: 30.9

Fiber: 19.1

Brown Sugar Peanut Butter Fudge

Serves: 8 (makes 16 pieces)

Time: 2 hours, 10 minutes - 3 hours, 10 minutes

Around the holidays, I always start making fudge. This recipe is easy to throw together and is a great dessert to bring to parties or give to friends. The brown sugar really adds a deep rich flavor I love.

Ingredients:

½ cup milk

2 cups brown sugar

1 cup smooth peanut butter

½ teaspoon vanilla

Cooking spray (for pan)

Directions:

Line an 8x8 baking pan with foil or wax paper. Grease with cooking spray. Next, pour milk into a saucepan and add sugar. Bring to a boil, stirring constantly, until sugar has dissolved. Stir in peanut butter and vanilla until smooth.

Remove saucepan from heat and spread into baking pan and chill in fridge for 2-3 hours. Cut into 1-inch squares and enjoy! Fudge will keep in fridge for 2-3 weeks.

Nutritional Info (2 pieces per serving):

Total calories: 335

Carbs: 42.6

Protein: 8.6

Fat: 16.6

Fiber: 1.9

Almond-Coated Truffles

Makes: 12 truffles

Time: 45 minutes

Want to bring something fancy-looking to a party, but don't want to do a lot of work? These are the easiest truffles ever, and will taste like they came from an expensive box. Simply melt chocolate, cream, and butter together, and then chill to get a Play-Doughy texture. Mold into balls with your hands, roll in finely-chopped almonds and salt, and chill in the fridge to harden up. That's it!

Tip: *If you don't like nuts, you can roll truffles in cocoa powder, powdered sugar, coconut, crushed peppermint candy, and so on.*

Ingredients:

10-ounces chopped dark chocolate

½ cup heavy cream

3 tablespoons butter

1 cup coarsely-ground almonds

Pinch of salt

Directions:

Put chocolate in a bowl. Pour cream and butter into a saucepan and heat on low/medium until combined and hot. You can heat in the microwave if you want, but be cautious and heat in 20-second bursts. When the cream and butter are hot, pour into the chocolate bowl. Rest for a minute, then stir. When the chocolate and cream have blended together, stick the bowl in the fridge for at least a half hour. Grind almonds into pieces. You can use a food processor if you have one, or put them in a bag and smash them with a wooden spoon or rolling pin. Mix almonds and salt in a bowl. When the half hour is up, go check the chocolate mixture. It should be harder, but soft enough to mold with your hands. Roll into balls and roll in crushed salted almonds. Set on a lined baking sheet and stick back in the fridge for 10 minutes or so. Enjoy!

Nutritional Info (2 truffles):

Total calories: 384

Carbs: 32.5

Protein: 5.9

Fat: 31.2

Fiber: 5.4

Cherry-Chocolate Nice Cream

Serves: 1

Time: 5 minutes

Whoever figured out that blending frozen bananas basically creates ice cream should be awarded a Nobel Prize. This recipe is endlessly customizable, but my personal favorite is cherry-chocolate. The flavors of cherries, vanilla, and chocolate are strong enough so I really forget there's a banana in there, and believe it's real ice cream. Because there's no dairy, it's a bit icier than regular ice cream - it's more like sorbet - so it's really refreshing on hot days.

Ingredients:

1 frozen banana

Handful of frozen cherries

½ teaspoon pure vanilla extract

½ bar chopped dark chocolate

Directions:

In a good smoothie blender or food processor, blend frozen banana, frozen cherries, and vanilla together until smooth. Stir in the chopped chocolate. Enjoy! If the nice cream is too soft, stick in the fridge for 5 minutes or so.

Peanut-butter variation:

Blend one frozen banana and two tablespoons of creamy peanut butter together. Add chocolate if you want, or leave it without.

Chocolate variation:

Instead of cherries, add 1 tablespoon of dark cocoa powder. Blend together with vanilla and add chopped dark chocolate, for even extra chocolate goodness.

Cookies 'n cream variation:

Blend banana and vanilla without cherries, then stir in a few crushed Oreo cookies. No chopped chocolate necessary.

Nutritional Info (1 recipe per serving):

Total calories: 218

Carbs: 45

Protein: 2.5

Fat: 6.4

Fiber: 5.3

Ganache-Dipped Strawberries

Makes: 10 coated strawberries

Time: Less than 10 minutes

Ganache, which is a blend of cream and chocolate, is one of my favorite things on the planet. I also love strawberries, so when they meet ganache, I'm in heaven. Unlike some chocolate-dipped strawberries which need to cool, these are meant to be enjoyed right away. The berries almost combine a fondue and a decorated truffle, and they're perfect when you need a fast dessert.

Ingredients:

4 ½ tablespoons dark chocolate chips

2 tablespoons heavy cream

10 strawberries

Toppings (dessicated coconut, chopped nuts, etc.)

Directions:

Begin by lining a cookie sheet with parchment paper. This is where your dipped strawberries will rest. Put chocolate chips in a bowl next to your stove. Next, get a small pot and pour in cream. Heat on medium until just simmering. Don't get distracted, since it won't take very long for just 2 tablespoons of cream to get hot. When ready, pour hot cream into the bowl of chocolate. Wait a few seconds, and then stir until smooth. Carefully dip in your strawberries, coating in ganache, and sit on the baking sheet. If you have a friend around, they can be responsible for rolling the strawberries in the topping of your choice. If you're alone, you can just do that after they're all dipped; the ganache should still be soft enough. Enjoy right away!

Nutritional Info (2 ganache strawberries w/out toppings per serving):

Total calories: 60

Carbs: 6.5

Protein: 0.7

Fat: 4.1

Fiber: 0.5

6-Ingredient Lime Mug Cake

Serves: 1

Time: Less than 5 minutes

Okay, so I'm cheating a little. This is technically a 6-ingredient recipe, but one of them is just olive oil, which you should definitely have on hand at all times, making it a little like water, salt, or pepper. I have found it is extremely difficult to make a decent mug cake from scratch with less than six ingredients (other than the recipe above), so here we are. I will sometimes find myself craving something tart and fresh, and make this cake.

Ingredients:

4 tablespoons all-purpose flour

¼ teaspoon baking powder

2 tablespoons sugar

3 tablespoons milk

1 tablespoon olive oil

1 tablespoon lime juice

Tip: *To substitute sugar with Truvia, use 3 teaspoons.*

Directions:

Whisk flour, baking powder, and sugar together a mug. Add in milk, oil, and lime juice until the batter is combined.

Microwave for 1 minute, then check the cake. A toothpick should reveal only a few crumbs. Cool for a few minutes, and enjoy!

Nutritional Info (1 recipe per serving):

Total calories: 374

Carbs: 57

Protein: 4.9

Fat: 15.4

Fiber: 0.9

Microwave-Baked Apple

Serves: 1

Time: Less than 10 minutes

Microwaving an apple may sound strange, but it's *way* faster than baking it in the oven. I liked to make this recipe with apples from the campus cafeteria, since they'll usually let you take a piece of fruit on the go. It's also a tasty treat with fresh apples from orchards, if you're lucky enough to live close to one. You're basically steaming the apple in the microwave, not baking it, so be sure to use a microwave-safe container and lid.

Tip: *If you don't have raisins or nuts around, you can also use store-bought granola.*

Ingredients:

1 apple

2 tablespoons raisins

1 tablespoon crushed nuts

Sprinkle of cinnamon

1 tablespoon butter

Directions:

Get out a microwave-safe container and its lid. This will be the vehicle for your apple. Cut the apple in half and carefully cut out the cores. Turn the apple and slice off the rounded side, so each half can sit up. Stab the outside of the apple halves a few times with a fork. Cutting the apple in half should prevent a fruity explosion, but better safe than sorry. Fill each core hole with raisins, nuts, sprinkle of cinnamon, and top with butter.

Put apple halves in the container and put in the microwave, setting the lid on top, leaving just a slit for venting. Cook for 3 minutes, then check apple's progress. After a total of 5-6 minutes, the apples should be nicely-softened. Enjoy!

Nutritional Info (1 recipe per serving):

Total calories: 321

Carbs: 46.1

Protein: 1.9

Fat: 17.2

Fiber: 6.7

Bananas Foster with Ice Cream

Serves: 2

Time: About 5 minutes

Hot bananas foster with cold ice cream is one of the easiest and most satisfying desserts I know. When bananas cook in butter with brown sugar, magic happens. The traditional recipe uses rum, which you're free to use if you have some around, but I personally don't think you need it. Just bananas, butter, and brown sugar, baby. Serve with vanilla ice cream.

Ingredients:

3 tablespoons butter

2 small bananas

1 tablespoon brown sugar

1 cup vanilla ice cream (for serving)

Directions:

Melt butter in a large nonstick skillet. While that melts, slice the bananas into coins. Add bananas to butter and mix with brown sugar. Cook, stirring, until bananas soften. Serve with ice cream.

Nutritional Info (½ recipe per serving):

Total calories: 328

Carbs: 35.5

Protein: 2.4

Fat: 21.1

Fiber: 2.9

APPENDIX : RECIPES INDEX

Milton Keynes UK
Ingram Content Group UK Ltd.
UKHW031823171123
432775UK00009B/457